The No More Gym Shorts, Build-It-Yourself, Self-Discovery, Free School Talkin' Blues

The No More Gym Shorts, Build-It-Yourself, Self-Discovery, Free School Talkin' Blues

Edited by Samuel Yanes

Harper & Row, Publishers
New York, Evanston, San Francisco, London

This book was produced and designed by Diana Shugart. The chapter "Lose to Your Muse" was edited by Cia Holdorf.

The type is Phototypset Garamond, set by Dharma Press, Berkeley, California.

THE NO MORE GYM SHORTS, BUILD-IT-YOURSELF, SELF-DISCOVERY, FREE SCHOOL TALKIN' BLUES

LIBRARY OF CONGRESS CATALOG CARD NUMBER: 70-168939

STANDARD BOOK NUMBER: 06-136063-5

Contents

The No More Gym Shorts,
Build-It-Yourself,
Self-Discovery,
Free School Talkin' Blues

Introduction

Gym shorts are not to be taken lightly; I have known this fact since high school where I was guided into enlightenment by coach Dave "Bull' Mac Carrell. Now the Bull wasn't a bad man, just a little too zealous in his desire to make men out of the pudgy young boys of Skokie, Illinois. One day, Bull decided it would be fun, as well as good for all, if I were to wrestle a big red-head named Ken Seeskin in a Texas death match. A Texas death match has about the same rules as a street brawl and doesn't end until one man gives up or is out cold on the ground. It was not my idea of fun, nor did I see what possible good it could do me or my chemistry career. The Bull, however, was not to be denied. The match started and Seeskin rushed at me with all the furor the Bull liked to see. My fight plan was to keep from getting hurt and still save face in front of the rest of the class. After administering about one minute of sustained punishment, Seeskin put me into a strangling bear hug. I don't know if it was a moment of revelation or merely a frantic reflex action, but I quickly reached around my opponent and jerked his shorts down below his knees. Seeskin let go of his grip and just stood there with red hair, a red face, and a red ass. The big hulk was blushing all over and refused to fight any more. Bull declared me the winner.

I consider that my first experience with alternative education because it was the first time I had ever felt sexy in gym shorts. Gym shorts are very comfortable, offering a lightness and freedom of movement that is rare in clothing, but their uniform drabness and unibody construction (they don't even have a fly) make them symbolic of an asexual type of education designed to create educational eunuchs. The main difference between public school education and the variety of alternatives is that public schools are not sexy.

I am not talking about the sensual physical activity we all know, but rather of that driving, daring energy with all its subtle loving and compassionate aspects that make for real living and real learning. Sexy learning has a power and a soul that stands out in a sea of dull imitations. It is a true and heroic process that can only be described as orgasmic by those who have tasted it. This energy is the great potential of alternative education, not the well publicized structural inversions of public schools, the so called "atmosphere of freedom." I would never have broken through the gym shorts stigma by wrestling naked, for I would have been beaten soundly. Freedom doesn't produce real learning; real learning produces freedom, and removing someone else's shorts . . . that's another story.

Samuel Yanes

New School News Blues

Harvey Haber

Harvey Haber started the *New Schools Exchange* back when alternative education was a fledgeling movement; in fact, it was Harvey who coined the phrase, "free school." I think Harvey's real genius, however, lies not in encouraging new schools to spring up, but rather in discouraging public education. A friend once said of Harvey, "He may not know what he's fighting for, but he sure as hell knows what he's fighting against."

If you look at the first few copies of the Newsletter, what it consisted of was that we started a project at the Santa Barbara Free School—a little exploitation of the kiddies, had them running this handcrank machine and stapling this newsletter . . . and then it grew much too rapidly. See there was a point where we could make a choice, say "Well it's too big" (essentially what Stewart's doing now) and just stepping back and stopping it . . . or else going on and doing a legitimate thing with it. Because we didn't have much sense of whimsy, we went ahead into legitimizing our thing. Around the 29th issue. And at that point we decided to take the big trip north and talk to the people about backing it and really doing it right. There were a couple places we went in San Francisco that I assume everyone goes to, like David Fuller at Eldridge Foundation and the Stearns family. There must be a ritual that everyone follows; you could see them from the air . . . By the time we got to Dick

Raymond at Portola, Whole Earth was already something of an underground fable, so it was with a tremor of excitement that we went to Portola in the first place. I had this stack of these old mimeographed things, and I said we wanted to do a clearinghouse for alternatives, for radical alternatives in education. That didn't stun him too much.

The function of the New Nation Seed Fund is to help new schools get started, and existing ones stay alive. (We have seen excellent schools founder for want of a small sum.) We ask you to remember this fund by thinking of it on your own birthday, and we ask you to send it a gift at that time. Since it is easier to remember small gifts than large ones, we ask you to send one dollar. If you are a parent, and do agree with us, urge your own children and young people to ally themselves with other children by sending small presents on their birthdays, fifty cents, or a quarter. We cannot solve large problems with these sums, but we can contribute to a large solution. Above all, we can keep alive one of our few working models of freedom.

George Dennison
Paul Goodman
Nat Hentoff
John Holt
Jonathan Kozol
—Issue no. 49

We went through old files and found old brochures and made some phone calls and got together about half a dozen pages of typed manuscript . . . I always typed it out and figured out what schools I thought were unique. Some of them weren't free schools at all, of course. The mailing list came from the first conference of its kind, I'm told, at Peninsula School[Menlo Park, Ca.] that year which was for directors and teachers at small experimental schools. There were about 200 at the conference, and it was a nice Spring day. It was a groooovy conference, everyone was very groovy, y'know seeing all their brothers and sisters there. Then everyone was just going to go home to their Suzy Creamcheese free schools . . . and nothing was going to really happen, you know, except this meeting we had. So we started talking about doing a newsletter or some media project to sustain communication between these various experiments in education that were going on, so they could help each other. Everyone said "Ray!", "Right on!" (no, they didn't say "Right on" at the time) and everyone asked for volunteers to do this newsletter. Cass wanted to do a publication . . . Everyone was going to send us five dollars a month, sixty a year, all these schools, and we'll do a thing. And then we got the mailing list from the conference and sent out bills for sixty bucks. Out of the two hundred there, one came back. And it was from Barney Young [Director of Peninsula School] So we had sixty bucks and we bought paper with it and borrowed some stencils from one of the mothers at the Free School, did an issue, mailed it out, and we got three letters back. You remember that initial excitement of getting mail? I wish I had those three letters now, I'd frame 'em. One of them said it's nice to see young people doing something instead of just talking. That's the one that tugged at my heart.

Don Frank, 550 N. Cahuilla Road, Palm Springs, Ca. 92262.
Next year I'll be in the 11th grade. Here is a list of the kind of place I'd like to be at for schooling. (1) Music—guitar and voice singing are the two things I'd like to learn most. Right now I'm a beginner at both. (2) English—creative writing. 3) Survival—how to live off the land around you by gathering food and materials needed for living. (4) Photography (if possible only). (5) The school should be out in the country near ocean or streams. I'd like to grow things and maybe have some animal friends. It doesn't matter if winter is cold or not. (6) Boys and girls who are free to play together. (7) Nice people. (8) Students should be given freedom and not be pressured. I'd like to be able to do the things I want to do when I want to do them, without having to worry about other subjects. It would be nice if it is a non-grading school. (9) No dress regulations. Now I know that there might not be a school like this, but tell me what you think I would like.　　　　　　　　　．

It sure is nice of you to help people find a school. I know, it's one of the nicest things that anyone has ever done for me. I really appreciate, appreciate it. Love, Don.

—Issue no. 35

As the Exchange became sophisticated, and dealing with these people, running around all the time, visiting and lecturing, getting into it, the ones you lost patience with were those people who had access to large urban centers and were still using the rhetoric of Waverly, Ohio, or were doing irrelevant, unimportant things and collecting money off it, because of this new found rhetoric concerning alternatives in education.

GREENTREE SCHOOL, WAVERLY, OHIO

We are still struggling uphill after spending a year building a little building to house 20 kids; a building that will satisfy the authorities. It has finally passed approval and we have been in it for three months.

We had a summer program with 7 kids! and have feelers out with a Welfare Department to get some more kids. Our school year starts on September 15 and we are looking for a teacher or teachers (married couples preferred) who would be willing to be a part of our diminuitive community and teach math, science, and or history. We would provide room, board, gas for cars, $50.00 a month a person, plus freedom to teach the way you want. Our kids are from 6–12 years of age at present though we take kids from 5–14. We need warm, mature people who love kids, like themselves and feel comfortable in their area of interest.

—Issue no. 12

Experimental education should only be undertaken under carefully controlled and supervised circumstances. Otherwise it may have adverse effects upon those students it seeks to assist. Experimental education is one of the most difficult and hazardous endeavors. I have come to this conclusion after a lengthy and involved association with the (blank) school.

Until such time as you choose to convey this attitude of caution to your associates, please remove me from your mailing list.

—Issue no. 11

There wasn't much going on, but there were some new private schools that were sort of liberative. First one I went to was the ————— School . . . There's a very large Georgian mansion, which must have cost $200,000 to resurrect and fix up, and there was a school, and it was all of those things—carefully selected, very clean-scrubbed black children in white shorts and pink socks and shaved heads, and there were a couple of Orientals, and a few other brown faces and a few Armenians, and a few white kids—a little United Nations selection. They had gotten private funding and they were getting extraordinarily high tuition from the few white middle-class kids there . . . Whenever you visit a school, the directors and the staff have a compulsion to show you the plant instead of the children. I mean, it's the same thing administrators have been doing for two hundred years, right? Free school people do the same thing: they show you their pottery wheels, they show you their darkroom, they show you the little kids' play area, they always show you the rabbits and the geese. But one thing I noticed right away because I'd been into free schools for a couple years was that there were certain clues to look for. I mean the walls were white, there were no scuff marks on the walls, no cigarette butts around the grounds, and there was just not much chaos. So I started asking about those things, what about the scuff marks? And it turns out that they do have janitors come in, and they are black, but he didn't want to talk about it too much. And the kids don't clean up after themselves because he had this big thing about kids developing responsibility later in life, this is the time to be free, when you're young, we adults can't be free. And then I asked him about the cigarette butts, and he said, "Well! Free children wouldn't want to smoke." I said don't give me that, if you don't let 'em smoke here they'll go behind that barn over there and smoke—and why make 'em feel guilty? And he said, "Well, I can't personally condone smoking" and went into this number about the evils of smoking, and man, I just got up and left. We were obviously both of us wasting our time. He was being totally dishonest and I was just being smug.

See, what it was, I'd been doing the Santa Barbara Free School since '67 for about a year and a half and I knew about other places, and periodically I would write away and get their stuff, find out what they were doing, and you'd come across bizarre little schools—experiments—before there was any Movement. One of them was a school on the tip of Baja in La Paz, Mexico, and it was some old guy who moved to Baja and got an old boat and he has a dozen kids down there and bought a little island and they have an old building in La Paz. One-third of the time they're on the island, one-third of the time they're on the boat, and the last third of the time they're on the mainland. And they run around, no electricity, no connection with the modern world, and they read Krishnamurti or whatever . . . and it was sort of a nice thing to think about, those people sitting on the blue sea, going to school.

YMCA, 1115 EIGHTH AVENUE, SAN DIEGO, CA. 92101. We are exploring the possibilities of developing an experimental high school as an alternative to the public school system. We are focusing on the needs of the fairly bright, healthy individuals who are being turned off by their present school experiences. We would like to know from other schools: What did you find your greatest obstacles? What approaches were successful in overcoming them? What approaches weren't? What things have you tried that you would recommend for others to try? What things have you tried that you don't think are worth trying again?

—*Issue no. 36*

It's getting harder to do 'em, getting harder to talk about how to start a free school. I mean it's harder to feel passionate about. See that's the problem when you're involved in a movement of any kind, whether it's self-proclaimed or media-proclaimed, and you're into it for a number of years, like Paul Goodman and others have found out, that you constantly are growing and you're expanding and refining all your feelings concerning words that surround that movement while the movement is accumulating new people. And you have to try to meet and cope with and guide all those people simultaneously, and you have this body of people, five thousand say, and this avant garde edge . . . and then there's this great mass in the middle that's growing geometrically, and they're just learning the rituals, and the routines of a new structure, and it's like . . . look, think of the tens of thousands of people who are going to discover the *Whole Earth Catalog* this year.

As it becomes recognized as a massive Leading Edge, like ecology the free schools movement will be courted by politicians, and made the subject of major rhetoric and some legislation. Its multiplication will crest well before the election of '76. With sympathizers it will represent a new constituency, small but vocal. And a hot political issue may be reaching public fruition at that time—the general proposal for States to issue Tuition Vouchers to students, parents, applicable at the school of their choice. At best, this could lead to an enormous freedom for new school and experiment—at the cost of freeing most of America to continue at will in racist education. At worst, by that early date, the Bicentennium, we may find ourselves, greatly disorganized, fighting out the question of whether the "free" schools will be honored in their freedom, or regulated by the government, censored and suppressed by economic legislation. It is not too soon for us to start cultivating some halfway-decent politicians, or generating our own, to stand behind at that time.

—Issue no. 52

This will be the last issue of the Newsletter in its present funky format. Next issue we are converting to a small magazine. The New Schools Exchange will still be the people's paper, but with more editorial content. The responses to the questionnaire which we sent out (and I want to make this crystal clear) have consistently indicated that our readers want more critical content. So . . . . .

—Issue no. 28

The Exchange could have been, months ago, a slick publication, and sold lots—fifty thousand each time—but like it purposely retained its image which is, by design, halfway between funky and slick. There ain't no color in it, and no gloss on the cover, yet it's clean enough and sophisticated-looking enough so that libraries will buy it, university education departments will buy it, research departments will buy it, and the bureaucrats will buy it. When we switched over to offset and the attempt at this new image, immediately we got 20 or 30 angry cancellations from grass-roots people who were doing little schools and were offended and felt, "Well, what is this slick shit?" . . . . They unfortunately went their way, and as it began to expand more and more libraries were buying it and fewer and fewer free schools were buying it, so we began to do a lot more running around and talking to people.

It's white (the Newsletter); it reflects the Movement in that way, in that the Movement is white and middle-class. We should call it the White Middle Class New Schools Exchange, so those reporters wouldn't call and ask all those embarrassing questions about chicanos and blacks. I really don't know what to do about it; or if I did, I'm not willing to make the change. All free schools have this problem at one time or another, their lack of ability to relate to third world people.

There ain't no Summerhill West no more. Director Frank couldn't hack LA any more, moved it to Hayward . . . and started Pegasus . . . from which he split to Europe and then a splinter group from Summerhill West declared they were Frank's old school and resurrected the ghost in Mendocino, calling it Mendocino Summerhill . . . zowee.

WANTED: Live-in, but non-institutionalized school in U. S. or Canada for 15-year old, intelligent, sensitive girl who is Ward of Juvenile Court due to rigid, punitive family situation that over years has led to girl feeling sad, inferior, directionless. She recognizes need for change. Counseling and close relationships needed with emphasis on personal achievement and tolerance. County will pay going rate. Write or call Mrs. Faith Apple, Deputy Probation Officer, Mendocino County Probation Department, P.O. Box 303, Ukiah, California. Telephone (707) HOmestead 24732 Extension 241.

—Issue no. 23

HAVER, BOSTON, MASSACHUSETTS
Haver is a place to come into your adulthood joyously and thoroughly. A community of learning: person centered, draft deferred. Call Boston (617) 523-2254 or write Haver, 49 Revere St., Boston, Mass.

—Issue no. 20

HAVER, 174 St. Botolph Pl., BOSTON, MASS.
Haver is a place to work on what is important to you—for people dissatisfied with their former/formal education and wanting or needing to discover and develop their own true interests and concerns—or, an alternative education and living experiment. The life styles and human-creative resources of Haver residents and friends and our communal living are offered as

tools for your growth—providing access for creative-intellectual-emotional development, in whateveer ways you can or choose. Come: for a month, for a year, or in-between, for as long as you decide—to Haver.

—Issue no. 24

The life styles and human-creative resources of Haver residents and friends and our communal living are offered as tools for your growth—providing access for creative-intellectual-emotional development, in whatever ways you can or choose to make best use.

—From a Haver brochure

How about Haver School?

That never happened.

You're kidding.

Yeah, that conference [Conference on Alternatives in Education at Zaca Lake in April 1970] spun off a lot of schools, people really got high; seeing all those people reinforced their uh . . .

How many people were there?

Actually about 2,000 came, 1,200 at Zaca. The land could only support so many people. Like a guy who drove here from Ann Arbor, Michigan with his wife and their cat. They'd saved up for two months so they could come, it was the biggest thing in their life, they drove all the way out, they waited in that fucking line for eight hours, got up to the gate, and here was that sign "NO DOGS," right? Because the ladies were worried about their deer getting hassled. So somehow it had been changed in Bob's mind (the gatetender) to "NO PETS OF ANY KIND." So Bob stuck his head in the car, "Any pets?" They said, "Yeah, we got this little cat." It was a kitten, about four weeks old. "I'm sorry, you can't come in, get 'em out, get 'em out," and he waved them back to the end of the line. And, bewildered, they drove back to Michigan.

Peter Crabtree, Box 104, Arvada, Wyo. MA in creative writing, dramatics and journalism, seven years experience teaching high schools, adult schools, junior college. I need a situation where my wife can work as I have two teenage kids of my own, and most free schools can't afford to pay enough for us to live on one salary. I'm tired of fighting the system and seeing kids permanently mutilated by the system; I need a job in a free school.

Jerry Schaefer, 613 Lincoln Ave., Lincoln, Ill. BA in philosophy, MA in Catholic theology, MA in English, with advanced study in Protestant theology and comparative religion. Am presently teaching English at a junior college. I would like to work in a free school atmosphere, at any age level. Have family.

Like this thing about being on the Dick Cavett show. You begin to think about that, don't you? Not that it would be a household word, but that it would be a word or a phrase or a series of considerations that everyone in the United States will hear about. I know that Agnew has said the words "free school" sometime or other. Or maybe his daughter.

You created the words "free school."

Put it in their mouths.

You put "free school" in Spiro Agnew's mouth.

I remember when we named the school the Santa Barbara Free School everyone thought it was a terrible name.

A few years ago, a nice man by the name of Herb Snitzer read Summerhill, *by A. S. Neill. He then went to visit Summerhill school to take pictures of it. Mr. Snitzer liked Summerhill so much that he started his own school, in New York, called the Lewis-Wadhams School. Two of the teachers at Lewis-Wadhams School liked the idea so much that they started their own school, called Collins Brook School. Soon teachers from Collins Brook School will be starting their own school. This is called a movement.*

—*Issue no. 22*

See, before '68, what did the teachers in the public schools do
that hated their administrators, and hated their principals? They'd
moan in coffee klatches in the teachers' lounge and that would
be the end of it. The unions weren't doing shit. All these
things—*Teacher Paper, Red Pencil,* radical organizing, *New Schools
Exchange, This Magazine Is About Schools*—they're all new phenomena.
Everyone, I'm sure, in these groups, is going through the same
kinds of parallel rituals . . . I've talked about it a lot, with myself
and with other people, and I no longer think of it as particularly
unique or charming, except for a lot of nice things that happen
along the way, and those concern meeting people rather than development and sophistication of the Movement.

There was a certain point when the excitement of moving the
printed word around was greater than the excitement of the Movement, like the processes of a publication, which was so new. Then
you have to ask yourself what it is that excites you. And if it's
the simple lusty power, then you have to worry about it. Not
worry about it, really, but you got to temper it somewhat.

Park Abbot, let me tell you about Park Abbot. He's a lovely
old white-haired man who has a place up in the mountains about
Bridal Veil Falls in Yosemite. He calls it Utopia. Kids from the
inner city, black kids who've never seen a mountain or a waterfall,
and he has them come there, they can stay there free, to see what
the country's like. He's so honestly warm, there's no shuck and
jive with his warmth, it's right up front, and he does what he
can do. He charges a dollar a day and he cooks all their meals.
He researches utopias, utopian dreams and utopian nightmares and
utopian fantasies . . . Before he died, before his ninetieth birthday,
he had planned to bring into concretion an actual utopian model,
and he died this year. And about two weeks before he died, which
was about a month ago, he wrote us a thing he wanted to go
in the Newsletter and he said, "Oh, by the way, I'll by dying
in a couple of weeks, so the mail will be forwarded to someone
who's going to carry on and answer the mail for me . . . I don't
mean to get all maudlin and make a big thing about this, but
it was really nice knowing you, and here's to utopia." Blam, and
he signed his name. And then three weeks later I got a letter
from his wife saying he died a week ago and that she wanted to

say that Park talked a lot about us and she wanted to get to know us some day. People are capable of the most extraordinary kinds of emotions. I think that's what keeps one into these things beyond a year or two, the people you meet.

A sound community would first need a plan that is civilized, and will work, and have longevity. "Civilized" should mean a community with social mechanisms inimical to brutality in all forms, and where human love is free to grow. "Human love" is the natural devotion to our species, and may have little or no connection to the immense romance of sex.

Any school where children grow toward adulthood with a wholesome capacity to love, should by sheer attractiveness, invite the children to remain and work and live, as they do in Spiro's Kibbutz.

Does this mean utopias? Yes, but good ones. We all live in utopias. In the colossal existing ones, ordinary people can't be full citizens even if they wish to be. In a continuing Summerhill my children and I would be full citizens.

—a letter from Park Abbot in Issue no. 20

Freely Naked at Pacific High

Jon Davidson

Jon Davidson has been working with young people as a psychologist for years, and only recently has begun teaching at Pacific High School, the free school's free school. As a therapist, Jon is unique; as a teacher, well . . . he doesn't seem to do anything different than he always does; that means unique. A friend once said of Jon, "I swear, the more he learns from his patients, the better a therapist he becomes. I think he's been going through a rapid growth period since he was born."

Memories of Pacific High School, written by Lloyd Kahn and Peter Calthorpe, are woven throughout this interview.

The main thing I want to concentrate on is younger people and your experiences with them at Pacific High. Everyone wants to know what it's like dealing with kids that age who are going to a free school, and what it's like from a therapeutic point of view, too—that's your expertise.

Well, I have approximately four weeks experience teaching with them, but there are a lot of things I've noticed and a lot of things I could talk about. In the first place, I find them tremendously older in some ways than the children in the public school system that I've come in contact with. They're quite capable of living a very self-contained life. They seem to need few rules, and it's not merely the fact that they're in a structure where there are fewer rules. They just don't seem to need them in order to lead sustained and creative existences. They do not seem brighter on the whole than the kids I've seen in other contexts. But they seem intensely more accepting of their own selves, and this gives them a feeling of greater wisdom. Obviously their knowledge is less in some areas, such as history and mathematics. The thing is that they're interested in something. It's incredible to me sixteen and seventeen year old kids who are interested in something beyond having to proselytize about it, they're *interested* in it. And it may be something relatively trivial, but they don't pursue it with a frantic urgency. They give themselves space and time. And the sense of time at Pacific is the most exciting change. It's literally like walking into another world when I walk from my car into the school, there's an altogether different dimension of time. Things go by gongs, and gongs come from people's desires at the moment. A class can spring up quite spontaneously because two people hit a gong and five people come to hear what the gong's about. And there's a class. Nobody wears a watch, somehow there doesn't seem to be very much need for watches at Pacific. They go much more by the cycle of sun and moon. And they seem to enjoy seeing what's going to happen in the next period of time which remains undefined. There's very little sense of rush.

What the place has been, despite what we write about, what will be written about it by educators, is a place where kids can come and live with freedom, do as they wish, make mistakes, learn what they want, or do nothing at all. Some have built their fantasies. There are no masterminds, philosophies, guiding forces, or directors, it's just a place to be.

When you stopped working with them at an individual therapeutic level and became a teacher there, did your perception of their education change at all?

No, I don't think my perception has changed. I just think it's become more intensified. When you're working with an individual student, you're hearing one perspective, you're seeing through one set of eyes looking upon a universe. Now I get many more facets of the same picture, so that the picture is not different to me, it's just richer.

I'd heard about Pacific off and on for a few years, knew that it was some kind of rebel school, that it was in the Santa Cruz mountains, that a lot of people's trails had passed through the place. Turns out that Pacific is what is called a "free school", not free to attend, because the tuition is high, but free in the sense that there's freedom from institutionalized education, it's an attempt on the part of the founders to make their own school. It started in 1961, went through moves from one place to another, heavy changes, finally was given 40 acres in the Santa Cruz mountains. The first school buildings were old tin chinchilla barns.

Three years ago Pacific high school was probably one of the freest places around. We had forty acres of beautiful land, a lot of close friends, some money, a daily influx of students, and no idea of what education meant or was for. Almost everyone lived in the flatlands and came in busses every day; it was like coming to a little haven of comrads, getting stoned and playing at everything from submarine building to James Joyce. In the winter the rain kept us inside and drove us mad with lack of space and dirt. People started hating each other. It didn't seem worth driving for 45 minutes to get a lot of intense conflicts.

Everyone had plans to make the school better (Pacific's greatest trouble has always been it unlimited potential) and all the plans involved firing someone or changing the government or embarking on some sophisticated program of cognitive development. The students fired all the staff, totally reorganized, restructured the educational process, and went steaming off for a good three weeks of scheduled classes and work lists.

An obvious observation about free schools is that the student's life is his education, and his education his life, even though he's in a school structure. I'd like you to talk about what that means in terms of traditional education and what you've noticed about that.

Ok. What I notice about kids in the public school system is that their drives, the things they want to do, the things they want to learn, are not related to the way they behave. It's almost as if they are being driven to do their thing. That does not mean that they do not get into it, and it does not mean that they do not learn a great deal—in some sense of learning, the kids at Pacific accomplish a hell of a lot less overtly, but there is a feeling of connectedness, quite literally, between the way they move and what they study. Between the kinds of things that they're tuning into and what they do all the time, how they are. In the public high school system, the kids I work with seem to have an external reference point, as opposed to an internal reference point. The kids at Pacific go more slowly, but they seem to see more, and in a very, very strong sense of the term, I feel they're more critical about what they learn and what they see. They don't know the rules of formal science like the public high school kids seem to. The public school kid will emerge victorious in a debate very often, but the Pacific student probably sleeps a little better at night.

Things started to pick up when the weather cleared and we ran out of money. The staff (we had all been rehired) that didn't care, stopped coming; the rest started camping out and sharing food expenses. There were less people around and less conflicts, nobody cared, really.

People had toyed with the idea of making it a live-in school but we were so lame and could barely keep the busses running and everyone out of jail, much less feed and house 60 people. It was the best idea, because everything we were trying to do to give students a sense of independence and autonomy was contradicted by their life at home.

By the end of the spring there were about 15 people living on the property and they were very high. There was no doubt that students and staff living in a community was the next step. We had a small kitchen running with a new cook every night. People lived in tents, parachutes, trucks, trailers and one beautiful house. The school was really on the edge of disaster; every time I went to the flatlands someone would ask if it was true that the school had folded. So there was nothing to lose (actually, I think that the "school" folded two years before that time when all those exciting things started happening in San Francisco.)

Speaking of sleeping a little better at night, an important part of education and therapy is sex. I mean, the sexual practices of a normal public high school student can be satirized; the student's life is a walking satire of sex education. At least

when I went, that was part of it. Can you talk a little about sex in free school life?

Sure. First of all, sex is not manualized at Pacific. The idea of a sex education course at Pacific is absurd. What there might be would be a student coming up with a particular question when that question is relevant. What is happening is that there is a considerable amount of sexual exploration, but in a very nonpromiscuous kind of way. And it is going on all the time, it's not confined to certain hours or certain moments, or certain periods. The most powerful perception that I have is that the people there are not obsessed with sex. I have not observed Pacific people making love, but my guess is that they get into making love with as great a degree of abandon as they get out of it. It's like when they're not engaged in some kind of a sexual trip, they really are not engaged in a sexual trip. It's an amazing feeling to walk around amongst a bunch of kids who do not seem to be playing sexual games with each other; no teasing, or flirting, or selling their wares to each other. It is an extraordinary experience, and quite frightening for most adults, I would imagine.

That's not to say that a boy and a girl cannot exchange loving glances, but that's what they are—loving glances. It's not all the other things that people do with their eyes in subway trains and cocktail parties and public schools.

You don't hear people talking about it, and yet you know when you talk to them privately that people are sleeping with people. But there is very little promiscuity; a relationship is a relationship. And while it's going on, that's what's going on. Most of the seventeen year old dudes get quite consumed in a relationship while that relationship is happening. In other words, you get longitudinal promiscuity if you want to look at it that way. It's vertical, but it's not horizontal; one person is not sleeping with three or four people at the same time, for the most part. Despite the complete absence of monitoring of their behavior or their morality, it would be quite far out for many of the people to be averaging intercourse of only once a month. On the other hand, there are people who are sleeping together nightly. Pacific is a residential school, people live there, and they build their own domes, and they live in their own homes; they create their own little world. And if a director goes to a dome, it's only to have a good time—there is no monitoring.

A lot of energy in the west in spring 1968. Alloy in New Mexico, Whole Earth Catalog beginning to click. A bunch of rock freaks dreamed up the Wild West Festival for San Francisco, rented an old Victorian house as headquarters and started coordinating with the mayor, Airplane, Grateful Dead, Panthers for a weekend of rock music in Golden Gate Park. We were going to build a 70 foot dome framework of conduit, put it up in a glen at the polo grounds and use it for concerts. Cameramen would be able to climb up and film from 40 feet in the air, hang speakers from it. Green paint outside, blue inside so it would blend with the trees or sky depending on whether you were in or out.

We were going in and out of San Francisco from Big Sur, getting materials ready for the dome. I'd met Jay Baldwin, who'd spent a lot of time with Fuller, and had dome building experience, and we were going to work together on the Wild West dome. On the way back to Big Sur, carrying a dome model in the bus, we met people from the school at Nepenthe—a lot of things in common, excitement, shelter's needed, here's a model. Later five people came to visit us in Big Sur, and saw the dome there; we decide to build some and start driving back and forth to the school. Martin and kids make a conduit frame dome, put together on a hot day with funky ladder and beer. School meetings are held outside under the dome framework. It's a symbol of what's in our heads. Sarah and I getting more and more attached to the people and the place, despite no place to live, no water, hot and dusty dry climate. We pitched a tent on the ridge, looking about 20 miles through the rolling hills to the summer ocean fog. Martin lived about 50 feet away in a pup tent, reading late each night by kerosene lantern. Fresh ground coffee and schemes at Mark's house each morning, swimming in the lake on hot afternoons. Problems seemed insurmountable, but we had nothing to lose. No water, no money, no unifying principles.

Lingerman brothers, sympathetic neighbors, brought their drilling rig over, and started drilling for water a few weeks before school began. At 180 feet, still no water. Martin threw I Ching which suggested we keep going and John hit water at 200 feet—20 gallons per minute. Jubilation!

The school was blindly on its way to becoming a boarding school. Not much was ever planned, things just happened with some kind of hazy group steering. It was too much of a hassle bringing kids up in busses from the valley each day and Mark and Michael started accepting students for boarding even though we had no place for them to live. All along, I'm telling them that a dome can be built in a day—the Bucky hype.

Are they freely naked in each others' presence?

They are. I took a guest down to talk to the ducks at the pond, and we passed a variety of nude boys having a fine time swinging on a rope and jumping into the lake. I imagine some guests would be upset by this. It's quite easy to have a casual conversation with a naked person there. But you know, there is absolutely no parade of nudity. It always seems to be connected with something like swimming or rolling in the mud or rolling down a field in the grass. But on the whole they're not nude, they're quite covered up. And there is certainly no flagrant display of sex for sale. Nobody wears anything one would construe as even moderately enticing. Clothing is rough and frontiersy and practical, and there's very little body ego trip, very little parading or posing, very few stances that I can observe.

There's always a lot of talk about, well . . . that perhaps the kids seem a lot more fucked up, at least on the surface, than normal high school kids.

Oh yes.

They are more fucked up?

They seem more fucked up on the surface. I'm alluding to your quote. Oh, there's no question about that—they are freaks. They're deviant to begin with, otherwise how the hell do they end up at a place like Pacific? They look strange. They let all their hair grow, I mean hair on their legs, hair in their armpits, you know—hair. And they don't like bullshit too much. You know, they really don't like bullshit. They do strange things, like when they're not enjoying themselves, they leave. And this is considered a strange thing to do. One does not leave when one is not enjoying

oneself. Right. One stays and continues the conversation, using a variety of modes of adaptation. But the kids at Pacific don't spend a lot of time adapting. They're somewhat more primitive, they come and they go. The nice thing about that, of course, is they don't resent you afterwards. When you meet a kid from Pacific, even if you had a bum trip with him a week ago, he's likely to approach you quite freshly because he's not holding on to very much about you. They seem to be more in the present to me. And people who are in the present seem strange to people who are not in the present. Whether you choose to call that crazy or not seems to be a matter of how you want to define crazy. If you want to define crazy as what a majority says of a minority, of course.

You see if somebody wants something there, they have discovered that the probabilities of getting it are much better by just asking for it. And this is not to say that they've got it all worked out, or that they're all terrifically together. Because when you hear their individual problems, and what's happening at the internal levels, you know they get fucked up just like everybody else. But for kids that age, they very rarely pawn off their problems on external causes. They're much more likely to assume responsibility, and in terms of growth, they're a light year ahead of the sciences.

Kids and lumber for the first domes arrive about the same time. Fantastic vitality. Energy. Movement. We walked around, picked out dome sites. We held an impromptitude dome class; everyone came. We went through the D-stick model thing, Bucky's trip showing the instability of the cube unless it has a tetrahedron inside. Started building platforms. Not even enough time to sit down and work out a radial floor. Lot of mistakes, but things were moving. Many people got in on the building; if they wanted to build a dome they'd come around and watch. We went into operation in an old tin building that had housed a horse, and was full of horseshit. We cleaned it out, ran in electricity, saws and drill press went into operation. As struts were being cut, kids would look in to see how. Everyone rushing to get their dome built. Things moving along of their own accord, no one directing. When I look back I see that what happened was a community forming itself, created with no real plan other that the need to live together. No grand design, no master plan, joys, tensions, both with the vitality implicit in beginnings.

We somehow governed ourselves enough to jointly survive. Community is a more economical way to live than a single family. One sink, one washing machine, kitchen for 50 people. An exercise in expanded awareness. Many problems. Your consciousness may change and then you'll leave the group, but if you can ride with it for a while, you'll learn fantastic amounts about yourself, and others. So different from anything you've done in the white middle class trip with all roads open to you from birth, color and poverty not wrecking your chances to do something.

The first dome was built for Steve and Sky, due to arrive momentarily from New Mexico. All our mistakes converged on the first dome. We never did get it sealed, and ended up shingling it with tarpaper and red composition shingles.

Maybe you should describe a little of what you do with them when you're there. In your class and stuff.

To tell you what I do is to tell you what happened. The first time I went down there, which was four weeks ago, I had three students. We met in a grassy field in the sun, and we started talking about dreams. The next thing I knew a girl was beginning to act out her dreams, and do a spontaneous Gestalt trip. And the other kids interrupted her and asked her questions. She got a little anxious when she got into it, and that was pretty much the end of the class. We talked a little bit about the way people think about dreams. We kind of visualize dreams, we conceptualize them as movies, you know—spectacular show out there. Not really taking responsibility for it. And when we started talking about dreams, these three kids really dug getting into the idea, "Yes, of course I dream my own dreams, of course I create it. Why the hell shouldn't I look at it as mine. It's not a movie."

So they dug that and they really got into it. And apparently they must have talked to each other during the week, because I came down the next week and there were about fifteen students all gathered in front of the store, and they wanted to talk about sex. But they really wanted to talk about the problems that they were having. So here were fifteen kids who had never worked together before, and one guy is saying, well, you know, what do you do with a chick who comes on like she's so hungry that she's going to eat everything in sight, including him. And once a kid starts talking like that, the other kids really get into it. So we started talking about sex, and about different kinds of therapy and how the hell you approach sexual problems. I was really surprised—forty-five minutes after we started, we were talking about behavior therapy and the scientific model of man, about Freudian therapy and the dynamic concept of man, and about bio-energetic therapy and the energetic concept of man. And we were talking about some of the implications of these views. What I ended up doing with them because it just seemed like the right thing to do at the time, was posing to them a simple problem: if a man comes into your office and you're the therapist and he complains that he cannot obtain an erection when he goes to bed at night with his wife, what do you do? What would you ask him, what would you talk about?

I came back the next week and this time every single person in the school was there, which just blew my mind, plus the director, plus the music teacher, plus two of the kitchen help. And I was just going bananas, I just couldn't believe all this. So we went down to this really big room and sat down, and we started with our little question of the man with an erection problem, and all of them began to be therapists and I was the patient. I was surrounded by 45 therapists, playing the part of an impotent patient. And I let them all kind of do a thing on that, for about 30 or 45 minutes, and then I said, "Stop. Do you remember what you've said? Let's go back and listen to the words that you've used. Let's see how many people have described my problem as an "it"—*it* doesn't work, *It's* too bad, how did *it* happen." And we started getting into how we objectivize in our use of language. There was this really fine flow, I really couldn't believe it.

We ended up talking a little bit about bioenergetic theory, and one person said, "Well, what do you mean, you can look at a person's body and get a feeling?" And I said, "Oh, I don't know, why don't you take your shirt off?" So the guy stood up and started taking his shirt off and grinning. People started saying, "Hey, far out", "Look at your shoulders, how come your shoulders are so up tight", "Hey, what's with you"—you know. But it was

a friendly thing. They were beginning to work, and yet they did not have that horrible self-consciousness that comes when you knock on the therapist's door and say, "I've got a problem. Help me." Right. When people come into an office, they talk about their trip, but they do not *do* their trip.

I've never really taught before, except for very briefly at Stanford, so this is all terribly exciting to me. I'm high. I'm just stoned when I get out of there. And that has nothing to do with the grass consumption there, which is inordinate.

Well, this is an extraordinary thing because very often teachers are so bummed out that no education is possible. Obviously at Pacific, you're as much a learner as the students.

The feeling of energy that I have after a day at Pacific is always greater than the amount of energy that I get there with. I feel that they give me a great deal, and they're not that open, you know, they're really soft spoken and quite to themselves. But you learn from a person not because he can describe his trip to you, but because in the process of doing his thing, it simply emerges.

John Davidson's totally prejudiced, but he also sees things which make him the perfect Mr. America. He is America personified. He can sit home and play a Bach concerto and cry and then turn on Howard Cosell and watch Monday night football. John Davidson and Sam Yanes should be the new March of Dimes kids, the red feathered Community Chest kids. Everybody's boy. Ha-ha-ha-he-hee-Hawwwwwwwww. It's astounding.

The place is governed by weekly meetings. With so many people, so many trips, there's little coherence. Half of the meetings are shoutouts. As intense as the joys are the problems of living with 60 people. Everyone is alternately loving the place and ready to pack and leave.

We knew we had to deal with the building inspector so we invited him up one day. We spent the entire previous day cleaning up, hiding the illegal shower; everyone was hipped to his coming. The place never looked so clean. We showed him Steve's submarine—Steve had been working

on it for a year out of oil drums, yellow with scalloped red fins, Cindy faithfully bringing him food and wrenches, kids with the freedom to build their fantasies.

Told the inspector we were going to experiment with domes. Somehow it came out in the conversation that an exception to the building codes were organized camps, and tent structures. Some research and we knew this was our only chance to build the domes. No freedom in California like in New Mexico, but there is a loophole. We decide to go ahead. We've got seven domes built by the time someone reports us and we get the inevitable call from the inspector. We're halfway within the law, as we've told them what we were going to do. With the Pacific High School fait accompli, and through maneuvers over the months with some good human beings in Santa Cruz county departments we somehow became legal. We've stretched the rules, but officials may not be too eager to close down a community of kids who have built their own shelters and are looking after themselves.

But you're aware of their age, and you're aware that they are immature in a certain sense because of their age.

Yeah so.

It doesn't seem to make any difference, does it? Goddamn.

Can't say that it does.

That's the amazing thing—is that you can talk about it and the tone is exactly the same as if you were talking about one of your groups of people fifteen years older. It's just astounding to me, since the crux of the public school attitude is that that's impossible. I can't believe it, even though I know it's true, it's still amazing.

Oh, it's amazing. You just got to start believing in the amazing.

I'd started writing a book about dome building in Big Sur after Alloy, and had stuff written on the sun dome, Big Sur dome, and floors. As we started building at the school I kept notes on paper bags, anything

lying around, throwing them all in folders. Our idea at the school was to have a group watch us build, then they'd know how to do it themselves, and later, they'd teach others, like a relay race, passing the baton.

Probably through the Whole Earth Catalog, *dome builders all over the country found out what we were doing, started writing, asking for information, and pressure for a domebuilding book began to mount. Obviously more efficient to take the time to publish, rather than write hundreds of individual letters.*

Wayne took over the building of plywood domes. Jay and Kathleen got immersed in building their pillow dome. Alan and Heath worked by floodlights. Martin got into a saga building his pod. Kids were frantically trying to throw together their own shelters. Seven or eight domes got built, different degrees of funk, in a few months time. As winter came we started writing, trying to pull our experiences together with everything that was coming through the mail. No electricity, writing at night with kerosene lanterns. Slogging through the mud in rubber boots (we get over 60 inches of rain each year.) Jonathan wrote the geodesic geometry section on a crumpled paper bag. Peter Ross was taking photos now and then as we built. Jack Fulton came down for about two days to shoot film, and printed most of the photos in two marathon days in the darkroom, doing the cover at about 3:00 a.m. the last day of printing.

Finally in March we had it as together as it would ever get. Stewart loaned us the Whole Earth *production factory, Bob Easton came up to help, thinking we were going to do a mimeographed booklet, and in two weeks we put together* Domebook One.

The youngest kids there are fourteen. And they're really schmucks. The things they're liable to do! They rip each other off for a little dope now and then, and they go into the refrigerator at three in the morning to get a snack, and then they have to do KP. And they do heavy things too, they really fuck up. There's been smack on the campus; there's hepatitis right now. There have been kids who have gotten really zonked out on dope. And I don't mean psychedelics, because I have not heard of a psychedelic casualty yet, despite a very high frequency of usage. But a year or two ago there were some heavy heroin problems, and I had to deal with a couple of people who were on heroin. It wasn't easy—they were like any other heroin addict. And there has been a significant dope problem on two levels. One is the use of dangerous dope, truly dangerous dope. Dangerous not in the sense that they're going to freak out, but in the sense of getting into a life style which does not permit them to have sensory experience, and which equates the nullification of experience with experience itself. I mean, it's still a tranquilizing trip. There's also been a problem in the community—Pacific has to maintain cordial relations with its neighbors if it intends to survive and prosper. So they have to be a little cool, and sometimes they're not cool, because they're fourteen and fifteen and sixteen years old, and they rebel, just like kids are supposed to. But somehow, my feeling is that they are in some sense less intractable. They still tend to listen and to hear and to see a little bit more. But if they get too far out on something like smack, then you can't tell any difference any more. You just can't. Smack's a great equalizer. And it doesn't make a goddamn bit of difference where you go to school if you get hooked on it.

Well, to what extent is the situation a result of the type of student who goes there, as opposed to the free school atmosphere?

It's a nature/nurture problem. Right? Obviously the kids who come here are, quote, different to begin with. But the structure augments rather than diminishes the individual differences. I don't think any kind of rational statement can be made about how much of the variance can be attributed to the trip they were on before they got there, and how much is a function of the trip they get into because they're here. The things that kind of bind them together are a sense of territory and community—they somehow seem to want and need that. And some kind of feeling for the process, as opposed to the structure of democracy. One of the funniest things that happens at Pacific is when they have to make their nomination for student of the year. You would not believe how they choose their nominees. Whoever wants to be a nominee—well, that's the most important criterion. A lot of people don't want to be.

I don't really know how come they're so different, how come you get such a different feeling when you're there. I know that in part it has to do with the structure, and in part to do with the people who choose to come here in the first place, and the parents who choose to pay for it. Pacific is a very expensive institution. Very few of the kids can be on scholarships because of the amount of money it takes just to keep the school functioning and alive. Right. So it's still not democratic in a sense that we do not have a representation of the real lower class, and there are no black students right now.

I don't want to give the impression that my ebullience means that the kids up there are on some kind of a joy trip. And that everyone's running around with big smiles on their faces and whooping and laughing and dancing and swimming and parading and having a jolly old time—not so at all, not so at all. They're just going around, just people doing their own thing. And although there are festive occasions, there are also heavy, heavy vibe occasions. There are moments in the school's history when its survival has been in great peril. And the feeling around the school is the same feeling that one might get in a tribe of people when threatened by intruders.

Summer hot and dusty, a lot of flies. We get the roll of aluminum and begin thinking what to do with it. Peter's returned from England, running around doing three things at once. I think I'll build a pod, no I'll do a triacon. Hey think you could stretch a dome, think it would work? Jonathan's conducting messy fiberglass experiments, calling Abe Shuster. There aren't many people around, it's relaxed and easy. But fall's coming and 65 kids to live there. Kitchen and dining room remodeling starts. It gets done like everything else, in about two months, half-assed and worst of all, not like the old dining hall which looked out on trees. When school starts to my horror, I find we've built a mess hall, like the army. Too many people on the land, the price of success. Mark, who digs farms and the country, senses it, feels the heaviness of so many people. The excitement of building isn't there any more, meetings aren't as violent, the juice doesn't seem to be there. Yet the land is still beautiful, land you walk miles over. It begins to feel like the time to move . . .

Rodent Cages, Trundle Wheels, and Other Basic Equipment

Skip Ascheim

When I first met Skip Ascheim, he was building some monstrosity out of miniature magnets at his desk at the Education Development Center in Newton, Massachusetts. I soon came to realize that this full-bearded, long-haired man working in the cleanest and most innovative of all the government supported educational research centers knew an awful lot about what kids like to learn with. A friend once said of Skip, "That guy will look at a big, ugly piece of mud and think it good classroom equipment, because he knows kids would like to play with it."

Before we start getting on a philosophical discussion of open education and such matters, I have to ask you a most troublesome question, one that has been plagueing me for months. What the hell is a gerbil?

Ok. Gerbils are Mongolian desert rodents which make great classroom pets. They are cleaner, less smelly, friendlier, more active, and more interesting than mice ar guinea pigs or hamsters. They don't need a water bottle if you keep them regularly supplied with a little lettuce and balance their diet with carrots, sunflower seeds, and some kind of protein food such as lab show or Milk Bone

Gerbils and other Story's

By Karen Ascheim

CHAPTER ONE

Gerbils

These are my gerbils Fuge, Fillis and christina

on the next page you will find out about my gerbils' life

At first I just had Fuge and Fillis, then they had Babbies (christina is one of the Babbies) Well anyway, after a while my father (skie) thought they were ready to go into a Dirt-Cage so we moved them. there were Six of them, and they were about four weeks old when we moved them. The next Day I looked in the cage and I found two of them DEAD!

---

and it was so sad that Dad said I could stay home From school that Day. Then we Dug up all the Dirt and found three other Babbies then I found the Sixth one (christina) in a Jar then I Took her out and warmed her up, cause she was so cold. Then we Buried them.

(the end)

CHAPTER TWO

how to rase gerbls

If you hold a gerbil up-side-Down then you can tell what sex it is if it has a sort of lump under hés Tail It's a BOY if not it's a girl this is what you would do

Never hold a gerbil like this, at the tip of the tail, cause the skin could slip off!

If you do have a Pair of gerbils, when They have Babbies move them into a Dirt cage when they are at least Six weeks, that's Why mine Died cause they were only four weeks. Christina didn't Die cause she wasn't under ground, she was in a Jar.

(the end)

CHApter three

what foods should I
feed my gerbils?

A good diet for your
gerbil would Be 2 or 3
MILK Bone Dog Biscuits, A
hand full or 2 of lettuce
and a small hand full of
sun flower seeds. Never

| milk Bone | San flower Seed | lattuce |

---

give your gerbil to many
seeds cause there like
candy to a gerbil.
and they will get fat and
lazy and somtimes
even sick.!

(the end)

ChApter faur

how to get gerbils
together

If you have
gerbils and you want
to get them together
Don't Just Put them in a cage
together Cause they may
fight! Put a grill in Between
the cage with one gebil
on each side or the grill

---

then a month later
Check on them. then Put
them to gether for a minute
if they still fight Seperate
them and so on. They will
get used to it pretty soon
they will grow to know each-
other and they will Be Lovers

(the end)

---

to:
   Sue, Rose,
Patrichaid, Donna
and BarBra.

THE END.

dog biscuits. Gerbils are apt to get fat and lazy and bored unless you provide them with diversions such as running wheels and things to chew. They can gnaw through cardboard, wood, plastic, even soft metals (like windowscreen). They love things they can crawl inside and through. They will be perfectly tame to handle if you get them used to it as youngsters, and contrary to popular myth, gerbil fathers do not need to be separated from mothers giving birth. A litter may have anywhere from three to eight babies.

Where do you keep the little devils?

A ten or fifteen gallon fish tank is one of the most useful things you can have. Besides being a terrarium, aquarium, rodent cage or some combination, it also enables you to approximate a gerbil's natural surroundings more closely than with wire cages and wood shavings. If you fill the tank one third to one half full of moistened dirt the gerbils will be able to dig tunnels which will often be visible underground through the glass. If the dirt gets too dry it won't hold together and the tunnels will collapse.

My mind is eased. Seriously though, I know that animals and things like gerbils are indicative of the open classroom method which . . .

Open education is not a method; it is an attitude toward children, toward learning and living, toward oneself. There are many practical and useful techniques which, if informed by an open attitude, can aid in the process of nurturing growth. But very often the same techniques or methods can be used in the service of the traditional attitude, which seeks to turn children into marketable and manageable commodities. There are many teachers and administrators these days "doing" open education who are really packaging the same attitudes in more fashionable wrappings. The message remains the same: learn to read and write and compete and do numbers so you can get ahead. People working in advisory capacities with teachers who say they want to change a less formal approach have found their greatest difficulty to be training teachers in new techniques, or the use of new materials, while not seeming to convey a new method. Great effort is made to involve the teachers in the process of developing their own activities and materials, in getting them to notice how they feel when they are involved, yet many teachers remain unswerving in their pursuit of method. Apparently many of us need it very much. As long as we need it, we will not be able to look at children and what they are doing except through its filter.

Maybe I should stop and give some background?

Sure.

There are two distinct lines of development which began to touch and interact in the later years of the sixties to produce the movement we are experiencing today. One is the phenomenon of Free Schools which arose when substantial numbers of people involved in the radical counter-culture began to have children who grew to the legal school age. There were hardly any real alternatives to the public school system, and small struggling volunteer-staffed schools have sprung up in many large cities and university towns all over the country, but most heavily on the west coast. These schools usually have a mixture of children of poor people, minority groups, white radicals, and even establishment-liberals. They are often started by people whose interest is solely the "lives of children" (the First Street School in New York, where Dennison worked, was one of the earliest). Yet very often a combination of pressures from parents and community and theory seems to strangle the original idea and replace it with a host of competing ideas. The topics of vital concern and animated conversation cease to be Johnny's fearful nightmare or Susie's map of the neighborhood; they tend to become things like Freedom, Responsibility, Basic Skills. The Free School becomes an Idea. Life, always recognizing where it is not wanted, slips away. The kids become instruments by which to test out various theories. The teachers who are concerned for children give way to educators concerned with models. Of course this scenario is not inevitable, but it is the kind of thing that seems to happen to some degree or other at many schools.

The other line traces from certain activities within the huge educational establishment itself, principally from the curriculum

BASIC SUPPLIES

Containers:

plastic bags
jars
bottles
cans
cartons (egg, milk, etc
jello molds
muffin tins
bowls
buckets
paper cups, flat &
    conical
glasses
pots & pans

Kitchen stuff:

salt
sugar
flour
cornstarch
baking soda
vinegar
glycerin
food coloring
soap flakes
vegetable oil
rubbing alcohol
aluminum foil
wax paper

*Counting & ordering
    things:*

seashells
stones, rocks
spools

peas, beans, seeds,
    macaroni

Recording stuff:

paper (white drawing,
    newsprint, oaktag,
    brown paper roll,
    construction,
    manila,
    bogus)
file cards
pencils (black &
    colored)
felt pens (wide & fine
    tipped)
chalk (white & colored)
crayons
tempera paint
paint brushes
grease pencils
ballpoint pens
erasers
clay
plasticene
plaster of paris
old newspapers &
    magazines

Building stuff:

wood (sheets & scrap)
cardboard (tri-wall &
    thinner, such as shirt
    cardboard)
metal
plastic

fabric (old sheets, bed-
    spreads, clothing,
    rugs; felt, leather,
    burlap, cotton, etc.)
styrofoam (packing
    material)
pegboard
masonite
chicken wire
screen
toothpicks
popsicle sticks
tongue depressors
straws
broom handles
canes, dowels
tubes (metal, cardboard,
    plastic)
pipe cleaners
sugar cubes

Household stuff:

broom
dustpan & brush
sponges
rags
candles
matches
all kinds of household
    waste (packing
    materials)

Fasteners:

white glue
rubber cement
wallpaper paste
scotch tape
masking tape
duct tape
straight (common) pins
safety pins
stapler (short- & long-
    arm)

paper clips
thumb tacks
brass fasteners
metal rings
rubber bands
string
yarn
wire
rope
plastic clothesline
ribbon
thread & needles
nuts & bolts & washers
nails & screws
hooks

Tools:

knives, forks, spoons
kitchen utensils
matt knives
hammers
screw drivers
pliers
scissors
saws
hand drill
wrenches
sandpaper
files
strainer
brayers
sheets of glass
C-clamps

*Many different kinds of
things to measure
time and space—
linear, surface,
volume, weight*

*Living things and things
to keep them in*

SPECIAL EQUIPMENT

calculator (mechanical or electrical; see Holt's letter again)
½" portable videotape system (Sony or Panasonic)
paper cutter (they come in the guillotine style or the rotary type, with the blade enclosed)
lamps, tensor lights
Polaroid camera

Transparent plastic storage boxes

filmstrip projector
overhead projector
35 mm slide projector
electric stove or hotplate (for candle making, batiking, boiling bones clean, etc., as well as cooking)
kiln (small 110 volt models available)
typewriter (preferably a used "adult" model, rather than a toy; also see John Holt's letter, p.90)

tape recorder (portable cassette models are more versatile in this day and age than reel-to-reel)
record player (be sure the turntable is adequately suspended so the arm won't jump during movement and dance; if you're into the $200 range, the KLH 11 portable may be the best buy)
16 mm projector
super 8 film loop projector

WATER & SAND, the beginning of you and me. Ideally, young children should have a chance to work/play with all three forms -- water, dry sand, and wet sand. Few classrooms will have the space to devote to them at one time, so you should think in terms of switching back and forth among them through the year as the children's interests shift.

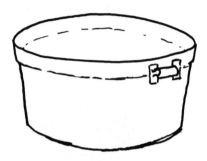

Galvanized tub from hard-
ware store, about $5.00.

Elementary Science Study Teacher's Guides on sand and water topics, available from McGraw-Hill. You can find the equipment for these units in the McGraw-Hill and SEE catalogs, but even without commercial equipment, they are rich with suggestions applicable to environmental and scrounged materials. The recommended grade levels should be interpreted liberally.

Clay Boats, Grades 2-8 (17562) $2.04
Colored Solutions, Grades 3-8 (17499) $3.96
Drops, Streams and Containers, Grades 3-4 (17692) $5.10
Ice Cubes, Grades 3-5 (18419) $4.38
Kitchen Physics, Grades 6-8 (19364) $4.20
Sand, Grades 2-3 (17683) $3.57
Sink or Float, Grades 2-7 (17724) $3.30
Stream Tables, Grades 4-9 (17731)
Water Flow, Grades 5-6 (17733)

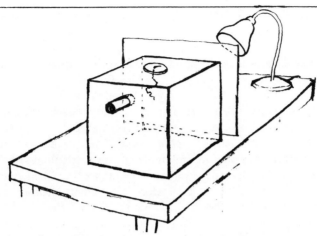

A SIMPLE PIECE of equipment for studying transforming of shapes can be made with a cardboard box with one end cut out and replaced with paper. Make a small hole in the top and stick in a piece of wire bent into any three dimensional form. Leave a part of the wire outside, bent at a right angle to make a pointer. Under this you can add a paper circle with degree calibrations marked, or just mark the box itself. Use a toilet paper roll for a viewing tube. When the paper is lit from behind it forms a translucent screen which will make the bent wire look flat, as though it were its own shadow. Turning the wire by its exposed pointer changes the shape you see. See how many different views of the wire you need to reproduce its shape. I.A. Richards calls this apparatus a Twiddle Box.

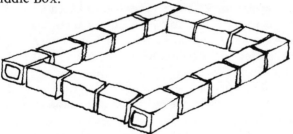

Concrete blocks covered with polyethylene sheeting or tarpaulin. Good for sand, probably not practical for water.

reform efforts of the early sixties. Curriculum reform was another one of those ideas which captured education for awhile. We can date it almost precisely from the day the Russians put Sputnik in the sky in 1957, a day of national humiliation for American education, for everyone dedicated to American supremacy in the universe. Educators, scientists, congressmen all agreed that we had failed to produce a sufficiently superior type and number of scientists. Federal money started pouring in, and countless curriculum reform projects were born. One of the most successful was the Elementary Science Study of the Education Development Center, then known as Educational Services, Inc. ESS is now in its final cleanup year; in its prime it housed a staff of some forty teachers and scientists and cost the National Science Foundation one-and-a-half million dollars a year. It produced some of the best materials and ideas around, really stretching the concept of pre-packaged curriculum to its open-ended limit. But the science units are not its most important achievement; in the course of its growth, ESS killed curriculum reform as a good idea and spawned a new approach.

ESS just happened to have a number of people who, even though they were committed to produce science units, were really into looking at what happened to children in school without a lot of preconceptions. What they saw, in the course of testing out their ideas, convinced them that the problems in the elementary schools were far more profound than anyone seemed to realize, that a poor science curriculum was dwarfed in significance next to the total deadening, indoctrinating effect of schooling on children. Along about the same time some Americans, ESS staffers among them, discovered what was going on in Leicestershire County, England. Bill Hull's article "Leicestershire Revisited" (Occasional Paper #1, Advisory for Open Education, $1.00) details their early, excited impressions. They found a state-supported system of some 250 elementary schools in which the prevailing ethic was not reactionary or even conservative, but an ethic of experimentation and change, supported wholeheartedly by the Director of the County Education Authority, Stewart Mason, a most wise and patient fellow. It became clear that any approach to educational change which tried to focus on one aspect of schooling rather than the whole experience which

Craft-Stix (popsicle sticks) *Constructive Playthings* $1.20/1000.

Tongue Depressors *Hammett* (92692) $1.70/500.

Pipe Cleaners *Hammett* 6" long $0.40/100.
 red (70777), white (70778), blue (70782), green (70783), yellow
 assorted (70776)
   12" long $0.75/100.
 red (70788), white (70789), blue (70793), green (70794), yellow
 assorted (70787)

Playframe *SEE* (XSEEPF) $78.00.

Tinkertoy *Irwin's Economy Store* (155) $5.95.
   motorized (177) $8.50 less 10% educational discount.

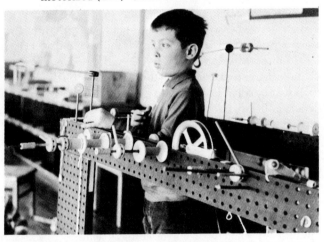

Elementary Science Study Teacher's Guides *McGraw-Hill*

Bones grades 4-6 (18495) $5.13.

Bone Picture Book (18496) $1.98.

How to Make a Chicken Skeleton (18497) $1.80.

Picture Packet (15 large skeleton illustrations) (18503) $6.54.

Changes grades 1-4 (17494) $2.73.

Clay Boats grades 2-6 (17562) $2.04.

Mirror Cards grades 1-6 (18417) $3.57.

Mobiles grades K-4 (17512) $2.37.

Structures grades 2-6 (17696) $2.55.

children are put through was bound to be irrelevant. Extending this to materials, the basic criterion is open-endedness, the capacity for extension to many applications. The aim is to interpose as little as possible between the child and the act of involvement, and the sense of a very wide range of materials is at least as important as any particular item or category.

These materials, though . . . what do kids get from them, or through them? You know—learning, asking questions, and so on.

Let me tell you a story, a true one that seems pretty dumb, but significant. A new teaching device came in the other day for us to look over, an inexpensive plastic hand-held box with programmed lessons on a paper strip inside. This machine is called Telor and it is a pale mustard color very like the yellow ochre they use on a lot of building exteriors here in the city of its birth, Palo Alto. Presumably this color is meant to recall the yellow-brown color of the grassy hillsides in the dry summer months. Maybe the people get nostalgic for it when the grass turns green.

My immediate reaction was oh, another teaching machine with a little window and seven apples and numeral 7 and a choice of *seven six five four* for answers. I have a thorough and unreasoning prejudice against teaching machines. Fortunately Hal was around; he took one look at the thing and said, "Hey, that looks like something kids would like to play with". That set me straight; the object in my hand wasn't a teaching machine, it was simply an interesting mechanism. There was a paper tape inside, and if you picked the right lever to push, the tape would move. If you opened it up, you found that the lever had a little hook on it, and the paper strip had little holes lined up with the hooks. The right lever had a hole in the paper waiting for its hook to engage. My head began to clear; of course kids would love to play with it.

The designers of these devices have made one very basic mistake, which may well cost the product its life. They all presume the validity of the behaviorist viewpoint of children's motivation, that "positive reinforcement" of a kind of behavior will result in that

Trundle Wheel *SEE* (foot) (ARN004) $1.75.
(yard) (ARN001) $4.50.
(meter) (ARN002) $5.00.

You roll it along a curved or straight line;
each revolution measures one unit of length.

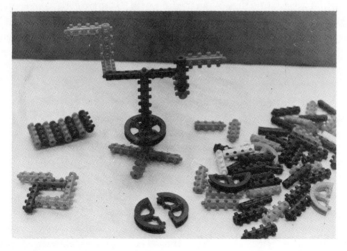

Playsticks *ESA* (7479/018) £3.10½ (about $7.45).

Soft plastic rods which fit together by pegs and holes either
side by side, end to side, or end to end.

behavior being "learned" (meaning trained into and adopted) by the child. It follows that "positive reinforcement" is seen as the motivation of the child. In all the programs for teaching which I have seen, the reinforcement has to do with getting on to the next problem. Success from the designers' point of view, is getting the right answer so you can get on to the next question. The fallacy here is obscured in most school situations, since they are structured to place the highest value on the students "progress," defined purely in terms of a linear movement along a prearranged sequence. So it is likely that the children will want to finish the sequence; that's the only way they will be approved of.

Of course the purpose of the program is only secondarily to be finished; what it really wants to do is teach its content, which is usually naming things or manipulating symbols. There are two different things going on at once; the child is manipulating the machine (whatever mechanical means it uses to advance), and at the same time he or she is supposedly mentally involved with the content. The assumption is that the child, wanting to move on, will have to pay attention to the subject matter, and since the only way to move on is to get the right answer, he will learn the right answer. Since getting the right answer is identified with advancing the machine, the adult assumes they are the same thing. But they are not necessarily the same thing to the child. We assume that there is some inherent gratification in succeeding, and we are probably right. But for the child, success lies in getting the machine to move on so he or she can finish. Associating the success with the right answers is a *learned* pattern, something we bring about by shifting the emphasis, diverting the child's attention from the mechanical operation to the content of the tape. In doing so we try to change the motivation from playing with the gadget to answering questions.

Questions and answers are a big part of childhood, to be sure. Children don't seem to have to *learn* to ask questions about things and to want answers. But in their case, they are asking real questions, questions which are asked for the first time, to which they don't know the answers. In our case, we ask them fake questions-we already know the answers, and they know it. We aren't asking to find out something about the content, we want to know something

Attribute Blocks (plastic)
  large set *SEE* (INVA00) $17.50.
  medium set *Math Media* (M206) $6.40.
  small set *SEE* (IN1278) $2.50.
  Math Media (M207) $2.60.

A 60 piece universe—3 colors, 5 shapes, 2 sizes, and 2 thicknesses.

Attribute Games and Problems *SEE* (AGCK00) $8.85.
  Creative Publications (MLM-42) $8.75.
A Blocks *SEE* (AGAB00) $3.25.
  Creative Publications (MLM-44) $3.25.
  McGraw-Hill. (18481) $3.35.
Color Cubes *SEE* (AGCC00) $2.45.
  Creative Publications (MLM-46) $2.50.
  McGraw-Hill (18483) $2.50.
People Pieces *SEE* (AGPP00) $3.65.
  Creative Publications (MLM-45) $3.50.
  McGraw-Hill (18482) $3.75.
Teacher's Guide *McGraw-Hill* (18479) $4.86.
  Creative Publications (MLM-43) $5.00.

After children have the basic idea of attribute sets down they can get into making their own; this is an important activity so that they aren't led to identify attribute work with a particular set of colored blocks. What kind of sets can you find in a collection of shells and rocks? Also use leaves, sticks, bottle caps, scraps of materials, etc. Stick shells and rocks to a remarkable substance called Adhere; the other side of it sticks to the wall. It comes in blue, salmon, or walnut.

about them. They are being tested *as people*; our acceptance of them is conditional on their performance. So of course they will become very concerned with performing. Yet we think with these teaching machines that they are actually going to care about the concepts on the tape.

Karen, my eight year old daughter, asked me to guess the names of her gerbils. I already knew the right answers, so I guessed them. She was outraged: "No, I mean guess some wrong guesses!" She couldn't of cared less about the "right" answers; she wanted to have some fun.

You have prepared tons of materials, good materials, but they don't really have built in safety devices for pre-structuring prevention. They can still be misused, and abused. What is the key for teachers in using the stuff properly?

We can take hope mostly from the overriding fact of nature that children don't need to be *taught* how to live in the present-that is their way. In fact, it may be the key to how we can apply ourselves as teachers most harmoniously to the evolutionary process we are sensing. The content of our lives is struggle, but we would be misplacing the emphasis and fooling ourselves to imagine that the relevance of the struggle lies somewhere "out there" in some imbalanced part of "society" of "the system"—that is part of the lie we were raised with. The relevance is inside us—we are the only "out there" that there is. And fortunately we, not "out there", are what our children need; the teacher as the person who shares herself or himself with children. No less than with kids, we need this too. To avoid the trap of living out our fantasies through the kids, we have to learn to open ourselves to them, not as the idealized beings the school system pretends we are, but as who we really are, with all our insecurities and all the things that make us joyful. We have to root out the arrogant notion that the kids need just what we have decided to give them, and we have to curb our own tendencies toward the messianic. We have to acknowledge that we are all the same species, that we were once "down there" where they are, (if we could only get back in touch with it), and that they will soon be "up here" with us. We have to

Dinosaur Kit *Edmund Scientific* (70,817) $6.00.

Dinosaurs are a great relief from geometric shapes. This is one of the most engaging bunch of them you'll ever meet.

Discovery Blocks *ETA* (1500) $12.00.

Rectangles, triangles, diamonds, all the same thickness; 140 blocks.

be ourselves . . . yet to say that does not define a condition, but a process. Being ourselves, after all, is what it's all about; if we are really alive, this will be *becoming* ourselves.

The Sense of Sharing

Robert Greenway and

Salli Rasberry

The voices of Robert Greenway and Salli Rasberry are very precious to alternative education. Their writing is always honest, always gentle, and always right for the moment. After reading their first book, *Rasberry Exercizes,* a friend remarked, "Greenway and Salli may be the very souls of the free school movement."

I haven't really talked to you since you finished *Rasberry Exercises.* The grapevine tells of a Seeds of Learning project you're on to. What's that about?

Greenway: What I started to do was to gather up some of the papers I had written and slap them together in a cheap paperback to send to people who keep asking me what I believe. That was a ridiculous fallacy. I wish to hell I had never gotten into it. My next mistake was to make an honest statement about where I was at . . . that was like falling off a cliff. Let me tell you the main structure of Seeds because it reveals a lot about what you probably want to know. There's a heavy section on metaphors and words, a heavy section on psycho-ecology, and another section on unfolding—the idea of man as energy rather than man as mechanism. I've worked on those things for years. My work has always been in metaphors and I am on to something because I know that the metaphorical way of knowing is the way we think. It's not just one way of knowing, by God, it's the main way. We all make our experience conscious via metaphors. Kids dig it, poets dig it, and the really far out scientists dig it. Most of the rest of us drivel around using the dead metaphors that other people make without having the bliss of making our own. I want to get into saying, wow, we're trapped between cultures or trapped between myths. If you want to know what to do in school, reclaim words, make them come alive again, come back to the mythical substructure of every word, the magic of all those wonderful ideas.

There are striking differences between sharing symbols and less symbolized experiences such as an object, an event, or time. Symbols themselves are out of time. The act of sharing symbols—i.e. talking together—is a shared act which is usually unsymbolized, unthought of, or unconsciously regulated. The act of creating a symbol, or fixing one for use is, in essence, an act of sharing with one's self. Finding a vehicle for one's sense of experience is like a paradigm of the sharing process between humans: an energy (from experience) builds up, some kind of becoming adjacent takes place. There is a linking between symbol and experience, some kind of harmony between energies.

—Robert Greenway, from Sharing

Greenway: What's happening now, what's happening in the free school movement is not worth more than a couple of sentences. What does Ivan Illich mean? That's worth about a small paragraph for me. John Holt is worth about two paragraphs. People like Peter Marin in his suffering are worth a lot more, not because he says good stuff but because his life is honest. The type of fucked upness that he lives through, I really dig.

How did you get here from your first book?

Greenway: The Rasberry book got it off for me in a number of ways. It was something that I put off doing for about ten years. Confidence is very important and I got a lot of confidence from that. The book worked. It was an honest expression of where Salli and I were at the summer before last. Looking back I can see a heavy middle-class trip in that book. I was still struggling with a school. There had to be a school, some coherent structure. I didn't have a real sense of the underpinnings of that book. Since *Rasberry* came out, I've been making a list of the foundations that went into it. I understand that people trust their own experience more that they used to. People are trusting private knowledge as never before. This is not a time for experts. This is a time for "what do I feel" and this has been bastardized and puffed up in the press as "do your own thing." I have come to hate that phrase with bitter passion. I hate it.

Hate your thing?

Greenway: It's a complete misunderstanding of a beautiful thing happening. Suddenly people are saying, "Hey, we are alone." You start from that and a strength comes out that got lost when we had the melting pot trip and superficial integration and all that shit. Black people reflect this when they say, "I don't know what it is but we've got to be alone." There's a flowering of individuality which can also be a trap. I learned that by saying everything I could believe in the summer before last. I also began to understand something about sharing as the opposite of competition. I wrote a sharing book which is a collection of poems. I knew that if I wrote a book of poems I would learn stuff. I don't have the last word on sharing nor do I live it completely in my life but I have to admit that I am conscious of it. That makes me live better.

"Knowledge"—packages of symbolized experiences—can work against sharing. Usually the teacher (reducing his fear, fulfilling his needs) works hard to attain knowledge, and to develop strategies with which to transmit it. He learns to stress (and create) differences between himself and his students. This leads to distance, a dependence on stylized roles, an aura of one side having the goods, the others not, a rationale for changing students. Thus it is that teachers, often inadvertantly become colonialists of the mind, the students the niggers, and the whole system in the service of the intertwining beauracracies of the state.

When people are viewed as deficient, the main means of changing them is to shape them into efficient receivers. Control mechanisms—forms of reward and punishment (sometimes subtle, sometimes not)—sooner or later implement heavy programs in the brains of children. In fact, the chief curriculum of most schools (including free schools) is not the knowledge which altruistic teachers obsessively wish to transmit, but the various control mechanisms they use. This primarily is what children learn. They submit to (and eventually adopt) authoritarian ways of relating to people, and these ways get linked to "knowing things."

If teaching is sharing, however, one enters into mutual quests with students, regardless of differences in age—a genuine exploring, building, searching, learning that both parties wish to undertake. The mutual trip becomes the dominant agenda rather than one dominant person filling a lot of empty vessels. It is easy to fake this approach. Teacher's colleges cover a variety of individual and exploration methodologies. These "useful methods," however, become more subtle approaches at control rather than genuine mutual searching.

Teachers who wish to share must accept the potential of full mutuality with a child. This means, at least, accepting the world of the child, his frame of reference, his myths and symbols—all this requires an awareness (if not full acceptance) of what did, and did not happen in ones own childhood. Amnesia of one's childhood, especially the years before logic and rationality, is well known. The adult must, in essence, recover his own earlier "culture"—the most difficult cross-cultural experience to achieve. And the most difficult of ironies: the means to do this, to recover one's own childhood later, is most easily learned during childhood, probably by example from parents who themselves are in touch with childhood, and can accept it without needing to control or dominate it. Such sharing within the home is rare, and thus even rarer outside the home, and the cycle of control, competition, alienation, exploitation, and "teaching at" children continues, and will continue until teachers realize the incredible benefits of learning from and with children . . . that teaching and learning are inseparable, just as love and sharing are inseparable.

If teachers wish to teach, they should learn to learn. To do both in any genuine way is to share with love. Sharing is always an exchange.

—Robert Greenway, from Sharing

How does learning fit into this?

Greenway: Well, animals connect directly with a need supplier and we call it instincts. They have a tissue need, a hunger need, a sex need, even a fear need. They plug in directly with their perception. There's a clean, direct simple line. In our romantic fantasies, Indians seem to do that. They seem to understand animals and harmony. We don't. We know what we need and we see the fullfillers of those needs, but we go on these weird side trips. You go to college for years and years, then you get a job, then you go to a bank and get checks, then you go to Safeways, and finally you get graham crackers. I see learning as the steps between our needs and our fullfillment. I have some kind of chemical need for my son to survive. I don't understand that too well but I know that lots of my moods and feelings and frustrations have to do with a chemical fatherhood. I want my son to survive. I do things that are relatively sacrificial sometimes for my grandchildren. Energy is needed for the steps between my needs and the fullfillment of those needs. I only have a partial instinct that gets me a little bit aware of what fills the need and then it stops. I have to learn how to make love. I have to learn how to get food. I have to learn how to survive. And learning is like little pieces of energy, but when we learn those pieces are spread all over the map. So I have a need and I have a little skill I learned in second grade, and another one I learned in the sixth grade, and another one my mother taught me, and I feel I want to get laid. So I go way over here, then I go way over there, and finally I get into bed and it's great.

By that time, you're probably too tired.

Greenway: Most of the time. We keep teaching kids irrelevancies and side trips. I see the term seeds as being really appropriate. They are little packets of energy. Free schools and free education now are really fucked because we keep saying, "What do you kids want to do." And they have already been acculturated through T.V. or Zap comics or whatever their hip trip is to ask for a lot of bullshit, too. They say I want to do this and we give it to them, but we are probably giving that guy a side trip. I want to find some coherent way to give seeds that any human can put together for a path that would be harmonious and thus more sacred.

Have you any techniques for this?

Greenway: I'm interested in looking for harmonies and I don't have techniques. I feel that I have a beginning that is worth saying to people and the beginning has to do with recapturing words. It has to do with every man becoming a poet. I see a poem as the most honest way you can say something, and it also has to do with harmony. Reclaiming words and getting in touch with natural cycles are an important foundation. I know we need more than just digging the sunset but when students in my class start to do this it challenges their whole life. They get tense, they get pissed at me and they can't do it. They say look, this is not a natural world, it's not Spring, life has to go on. My philosophy is that if we get in touch with natural cycles, when we get back to technology we will be purer. We'll be more sacred. I would reclaim words because they are so crucial in the time-bind that we are in. Kids do it naturally. Adults have to do it so that at the very least they don't take it away from kids. You ought to hear my son's poetry.

Salli: The way he reads . . . He's being Greenway, only he can do it much more innocently.

Greenway: "I was on the beach/ the sun was setting/ I tried to catch the gold." I've said that, but shit, it never sounded like that. It was so pure and fine. We have a poetry group every Wednesday night and he sort of got into it. He tried out a little one liner; nobody jumped on it. A few people said, "Far out, Eric." So the next week he tried about five lines, and he got a lot of acclaim and really tripped out on it. So the next week he came in with three full pages of wild, weird, personal experiences, and everyone freaked out.

I always knew he was a poet.

Salli: Everyone said he was but they were trying to make excuses for him being so spaced out.

Greenway: It changed my relationship with him because now I feel super confident in our silences. I used to always try to think of things to say, which was fucked.

Salli: Since we all decided to be separate human beings each one of the kids has gotten into far out trips.

Greenway: You're into teepees, I'm into sex, Eric's into poems. . .

Salli: Hey I thought I was into sex. You mean you're into sex too.

Greenway: That's my trip, you can't do it.

How about sex education?

Salli: I'll tell you how my class started. I had been thinking about how to introduce sex education in the school but I couldn't bring myself to just going in and saying, "Hey let's talk about sex."

Greenway: Without getting put into jail.

Salli: One day I was down at the barn and I went in and climbed in the hay loft. I looked down and the kids had followed me but were afraid to come in because they knew it was my space. They were peeking in and I was wondering if they would come in. They couldn't come in the front door so they went around to the way the animals come in and they all gathered around and looked up at me. It was real cozy.

Greenway: They knew it was time for the sex class.

Salli: But I never had said it. They just knew.

Greenway: That's the basis of all good teaching when the kids know what you're into. They pick you.

Salli: They asked questions like, "What's it like to fuck?" and "We want to see you fuck." I said, "Well . . ." and left it. The first two meetings I talked about having babies and all that. Finally they said, we already know that, we just want to see people fuck. Almost all of the kids had sneaked in to see their parents. And they know when it is happening but they don't feel part of it. They want to very much. I asked them if they wanted to fuck. One boy, ten years old, said he wanted to very much but that no one was interested in him. I told them they could see the movies but I couldn't get into making love in front of them. They kiss me now and the boys pretend to bump up against me and touch my breasts.

Greenway: Cop a feel, huh. My music teacher used to stand up behind me when I was playing the piano and sometimes she would be really excited because I was really good and she would rub up and against my back and I would sit there trying to do it through my backbones.

Salli: That's what they do. One of the parents said why don't you turn them on to animals . . . because they were uptight about the whole thing. So we looked at . . .

Turn them on to animals?

Salli: They're all fucking sheep in Bodega Bay. No, I've been taking them around watching the sheep. They look at pregnant cows and things like that.

Greenway: I can see them staring at the genitals of a poor defenseless sheep.

Salli: Really what the kids want is a way of being close to adults. Now we're talking about jealousy, competition, possessiveness . . . Things that no one told us about. I think its groovy. Anybody can fuck, its the relationship part that gets screwed up. That's what my focus is.

Greenway: I was disturbed for about ten years by pictures of women's bodies cut in half showing the different holes. Think of how tragic it is to link that with sex. My son Steven and his friend are thirteen and they are just like horny loggers all the time now. They laugh at their awkwardness. They're trying to get a girl from the free school over to the house for the weekend. They'll freak out if they ever do because they don't know quite what to do . . . they sort of do . . . they'll take a sauna . . . I don't know what they'll do. They argue with each other over approach. Steven says, "we shouldn't come on straight, we should talk to her until she trusts us. Andy says no, "Do you want to come over and fuck or not," that's what I'm going to say.

Let me tell you how all these learning theories fit together.

OK.

Greenway: It starts with energy exchange. It's the idea that every word is like a seed of energy. And every idea is a fantastic cluster of seeds of energy. When you transmit that to someone you can have an energy loss. You have to be careful about not spending your capital, but just transmitting the overflow. Energy theory fits into Zen and Hindu stuff and it is also fun as hell. Thinking of people as energy clusters gets into sharing. I can share with an energy cluster but I can't with a mechanism. I can see you as a transformer of energy from the sun and from plants and occasionally from a hamburger that you eat. I can understand food better and see where food fits into all the changes. I can see where the myths fit in when I translate everything that I know into energy. Remember the movie, 2001. There's an image that says it mythically from that movie. There's a time trip that happens in that movie. Salli and I dropped a well known psychedelic that shall remain nameless and went to see the movie. I had seen it four or five times, but Salli hadn't seen it. I told her, "this is so long, but don't be bored." You know, I gave her the introductory rap. We got in there and the movie went like this. Snap. I've never been through such a fast, speedy experience. Wow. We got out of the thing and could hardly walk. We went outside and walked right into the sheriff's car. Couldn't drive home hardly, but we got there and Salli said, "Ooohh, look at the sky." The stars were going over in bands.

Salli: We thought we were lying down, but we were standing up.

Greenway: I said, "It's OK, we'll figure it out in a minute," and it finally dawned on me that the fog was blowing in in bands across the stars. Anyway, in that movie, the satellite is turning around a big giant thing in beautiful circles and a spaceship is coming up from earth. It comes into the satellite that is turning and all of a sudden it stops and starts turning with it. For sharing to take place there has to be a getting into parallel. And for teaching as sharing rather than teaching as mind-fucking the two people have to be parallel, they have to get in harmony. Only then can you put out messages that are free.

Unfolding brings it together. Children unfold and recapitulate their ancient history. Every child as he grows from conception on is recapitulating ten million years of evolution. We forget the power of that. And one of the main things of teaching and learning is simply to provide space for unfolding. The child is unfolding through eons and eons of seeds of energy. And there are critical periods of unfolding. There is a time to learn music most effectively. This provides a base to say, Ok, I see what I owe my child; I see enough of what I believe in and now I can get it on to transmit that to him.

I think that a learner is a person who has a flow open either between people or his own ground of being and his consciousness. And that flow, for me, is becoming more and more synonymous with love. When that flow is wide open and not distorted, you learn from your bones . . . its like making love to your own ancient history.

The Bead Game

Peter Lynn Sessions

Peter Sessions is a genius. All he has done with his experimental music program at Portola Institute, has been to recapture the harmonics of Pythagoras and apply those principles to a curriculum model that could revolutionize education. After taking one of Pete's classes for a few months, a friend said, "I wandered in hoping to learn how to play a little piano, but I've come out with a small understanding of what it is all about, and I do mean *all* about."

Then is, as now, a time of song.
And here is the wand
Of song, waving downward,
For nothing is common. It awakens
The dead, those not yet imprisoned
By coarseness. There wait however
Many with shy eyes, thirsting,
To see the light . . . .

—Holderlin, "Patmos"

To me, the most fascinating part about your work is that you make music education seem more conducive to real learning than most subjects. I wonder if you could talk about this? What makes music so universal and important?

There are a lot of reasons why you could consider music important. First, because it is fun. It's one of the more fun things you can do. Just humming a tune using your natural music apparatus, or listening to music, really listening like you do when you are in a heightened state of consciousness, is a form of communication with yourself and with others that is very personal and very abstract. And music theory as a mental discipline is about the most theoretical and abstract subject that you could ever get into, and yet it's completely accessible even to the most beginning student. In music you have the reality of a real sound structure that's accessible and instruments that are easy to play, like the electronic organ. It's a cinch.

I've also found that in the little jumps ahead, in attempts to program my mind by autosuggestion, there is a level of mind that can best be described as pure tones, which may account for a lot of the effect that music has on people. It is a language that your mind uses to talk to itself or to describe or code some function. I haven't exactly found out at what level that language is, but I do know that by imagining pure tones I can locate the level of consciousness in my mind. When I am in a trance state and listening to music, I can discover—in a literal sense uncover, a level of functioning in my mind which I was never aware of before, and consciously perform actions on that.

It goes without saying that we never perceive the spheres of pure elements, and that all our perceptions apply to states of matter in which one element predominates without the others being completely absent. The fact that in practice we do not perceive external sounds except through vibrations of other elements, is merely a deficiency of our external organs and doesn't change the fact that, even thus limited, hearing remains the only direct perception we have of a pure vibratory state. The other senses produce perceptions of vibratory states which are more and more complex and therefore more difficult to understand and to analyze. The vibrations of sound are the forms of perception closest to the primary state of cosmic manifestation. The vibratory states which give birth to the world cannot be differentiated from thought. Creation is conceived as a mental vibration, which is the thought of the universal being, and which composes a world which is nothing but a manifestation of mental energy; a thought which appears as a reality precisely because of the limits of sensory perception of the individual consciousness of living beings. Sound, even in its grossest, most limited form, is not only the vehicle of thought but the image of its intrinsic nature. For this reason through the intermediary of sound, through the Word, the utterance, knowledge is expressed, revelations are made manifest. And by sound also, all thought is conditioned, formed, and fashioned. Sound is the instrument of all development. The effect of sound upon human consciousness is therefore fundamental.

—Alain Danielou, "The Influence of Sound Phenomena On Human Consciousness"

It seems that music with its principles of symmetry and harmony provides the key to a kind of education that is almost impossible any other way.

That's right. You immediately reach a very high level of abstraction, and yet one that is very concrete. You can meet the needs of as many learners as you have. If you can get over hang-ups about having to memorize everything, you can have an incredible lot of fun, which to me is the main point of life or education—to learn how to have fun on this plane.

What about some of those hang-ups?

I started the music education program after teaching guitar and some other instruments for about ten years. In the last five years or so I started to get into music theory, which I learned in the traditional way. I taught myself out of books and learned how to read the notation. I gradually accumulated a vocabulary, but soon realized there wasn't much more than what other people had said, what they decided was important to put into a book. Look, this technique exists. It was inductive rather that deductive, and it involved memorizing a notation system and then memorizing a bunch of terms and then memorizing a bunch of examples. There were very few attempts to generalize beyond specifics. It was just mainly a naming system for what had occurred, and as such, it was very difficult to teach people. On the other hand, anytime I would try something that was deductive—try to use a general principle and get people to work deductively from it—I found that they had been programmed in school to accept only memorized types of approaches. Trying to work back and forth, I soon discovered that the first thing I had to do in teaching music the way I felt it would really benefit people most, was to free them from their desire to memorize—teach improvization, to reject all attempts to memorize, and make it virtually impossible for anybody to get anything out of the instructions given if they just tried to memorize it. Now things like the Finger Pickin' Dominoes and stuff like that are just applications of that desire. There is nothing in there to memorize except the very basic units, and past that point the student just has to make up his own patterns. There are a few examples given but mostly it's a forced improvizational process. You have to put it together your own way, and I really like that.

In other words, patterns are there just waiting to be discovered.

Right. Dewey and other thinkers put out the idea that it was the energetic process that caused learning to occur, that the person himself did whatever it was that was to be done, that activity was the energy which the person himself put in to create the learning experience. So far there are two ways to approach that, and one of them has gotten most of the news. That's the inductive way in which a problem situation is presented. There's something problematical about that, however. The student, the learner, is asked to create a concept, to act and put in energy from a real-life thing to a concept that explains it. That's what the inquiry approach and other related approaches are all about. They're inductive. All the teacher has to do is to check and see that the made-up concept conforms to reality, and the student is able to justify what he has done.

But that's only half of what could be done. When presented with a question from one of his disciples, a guru almost always gives the correct answer. But it is so abstract that the student just doesn't understand it. And only later, when the disciple has put enough of himself into the problem does he realize, "My God, that was the answer and it was there in front of me for all this time." Pattern learning, which is what I have been working on,

finger-pickin' dominoes...

FINGER PICKIN' DOMINOES is a system to teach you how to play the right hand finger picking patterns characteristic of Folk and Country guitar music.

You will start by learning to play the basic units (beats) and then proceed to arrange these units into repeating patterns of four beats each.

The information or skill represented by each box on this chart must be mastered before proceeding to the next. Have fun!

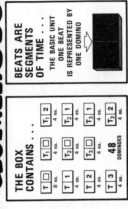

RIGHT HAND

1 2 3

T

THE BOX CONTAINS . . .

T □	8 ea.			
T 1	4 ea.		T₁ □	4 ea.
T 2	4 ea.		T₂ □	4 ea.
T 3	4 ea.		T₃ □	4 ea.
			T₁ 2	4 ea.
			T₂ 1	4 ea.
			T₃ 1	4 ea.
			T₃ 2	4 ea.

48 DOMINOES

THE THUMB (T) STRIKING A SINGLE BASS STRING MARKS THE BEGINNING OF ONE BEAT . . .

A ROW OF DOMINOES STANDS FOR A SERIES OF BEATS . . .

BEATS ARE SEGMENTS OF TIME . . .

THE BASIC UNIT ONE BEAT IS REPRESENTED BY ONE DOMINO

ANY BEAT MAY BE DIVIDED IN HALF . . .

A FINGER PLUCKING A SINGLE TREBLE STRING AS INDICATED BY THE 1, 2, and 3 IN THE DIAGRAM MARKS THE BEGINNING OF A HALF BEAT . . .

△ WHOLE BEAT △

T 1

INDEX FINGER
◁ HALF BEAT ▷
THUMB

T 2

SECOND FINGER
THUMB

T 3

THIRD FINGER
THUMB

THUMB   FINGER

A FINGER MAY PLUCK AT THE BEGINNING OF A BEAT ALONG WITH THE THUMB . . .

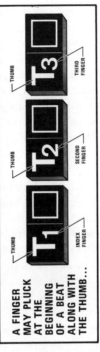

THUMB

T₁ □   INDEX FINGER

T₂ □   SECOND FINGER

T₃ □   THIRD FINGER

FINGERS MAY PLUCK TWICE IN ONE BEAT . . .

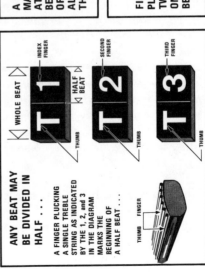

SECOND FINGER
THUMB
T₁ 2   INDEX FINGER

T₂ 1
T₃ 1
T₃ 2

really is an attempt to make the second approach accessible as a learning tool for people who are interested in the broader implications of what discovery learning means. There can be a deductive side to discovery learning, where the student discovers how to take higher order abstractions and make them concrete in the same way that the teachings of a guru are of a high pattern order, but still the truth. It works because the student still has to put in his own energy, and it's not the same old given formula followed by two or three examples which a student memorizes and is taught only application skills. Pattern learning literally works on the process of how knowledge is created from pattern. The idea of an interaction between the natural properties of vibrating objects with the idea of symmetry could be derived inductively, but to get some of the patterns we've discovered would be unlikely for most students even working a lifetime. And so I've found it just as effective in a learning sense to present these higher order patterns, using numbers to represent tones as patterns. And then, without having to do any examples, let the student wrestle with the problem of how to rationalize, how to develop the implications of this for his own creative activity. It's in that process that the learning really occurs. I've seen it.

If we listen to ourselves, and test the manifold feelings, wishes and thoughts of our psychic power, for a state of mind which leaves old things in their truth while joining the new in a natural continuation to the old, then we shall find, I believe, two spiritual forms out of which the old can be revived, and the new can be begotten in the womb of past cultures. These two forms of the spirit, so it seems to me, we can best name with the terms measure *and* value: *measure as a term for the order of things, value as a term for the law of things. Measure and value however are two psychic principles, two spiritual categories in which, since ancient times, a very specific mode of thinking has moved: that of* harmonics.
—Hans Kayser, from Akroasis

How do you teach for that effect?

The teaching involves the book, the tool itself, the *Bead Game*, and the class which is the core of the experiment. That's been going on for about two years now. And it was out of the questions raised in that activity that a lot of this other stuff came out. I had been a professional musician, not a learning theorist; I knew nothing at all of learning theory, and I wasn't aware of how what I was doing related to anything anybody else had done in that area. As I started to teach, I soon came to realize that there were patterns to the way in which people approached learning. In teaching somebody how to pick a convincing sounding blues, I became aware that there were habits that people used frequently that kept them from learning what they were trying to learn. During the first few years of my career as a music teacher, I had maybe two or three students at a time. During 1968 and 1969, though, I had as many as sixty different students every month. By this time I was really paying attention to where their heads were at when they started taking lessons.

I wish I had movies of some of those sessions. I would present somebody with a real pattern, so simple it didn't need to be memorized. All the knowledge following from it follows like leaves falling from a tree. If they didn't get that immediately they fell back on memorization, and you can tell you've blown it. There's a point in learning, in the beginning when you introduce the subject, where the pupils of the student's eyes are large. At the moment at which you blow it and they say "Oh—oh, I'm not going to get this this way" there is a narrowing of the pupil—you can see it, and it's at that point that they will begin to memorize. It's one hundred per cent diagnostic. It happens every time . The minute someone says "oh—oh," they get that familiar feeling of insecurity as a learner and the pupils of their eyes go whinng. It's almost the opposite of the danger situation response.

I found that what I had to do was begin working on some techniques for breaking through that kind of response, because I really think that there has to be a higher order theory about how people learn that is very, very different from the way that people conceive of learning theory right now.

After a nice public school education you are beautifully conditioned not to have any feeling of power as a learner. What I've been trying to do with my experiments is to say there must be a way to bring them of out of that predicament. I'm not willing to accept it and to say, "Well, that's what happens." So I started working on some techniques for getting people into different things, and that's what the classes were mainly about. Once I had learned in the first few classes that the ideas themselves were valid, I immediately began experimenting with ways of getting people to look at learning in a different way and I came to understand how I could help people do this by learning in a different way myself. I developed an informal learning theory of my own that works, something like this: learning is a biological process of growth and change, and thus it is like any other biological process—it is energy controlled.

It has to do with the channeling of energy to parts of your body. I don't see any difference between this approach and the notion of chakras. I think it's essentially the same insight. Now, most of the students I teach would not be willing to subject themselves to the rigorous discipline that it takes to control the energy centers in the body. And I think it is kind of a shame, but in the world we have there are few teaching roots or teachers who understand the necessity of putting all the domains of human possibility together. The three domains we have here are the cognitive, the psycho-motor, which is basically perception and motor skills, and the affective, which is attitudes and feelings. Plato said that in order to really gain control over any one of these they have to be integrated, all three together in a fourth domain, the spiritual domain—pure knowledge.

We have to treat man as an organism, but a certain kind of organism. And it's the energy that controls what you learn. The directing of energy to tissues is in fact learning. Motivation is energy which is available for such a change, and may be made available by being part of a plan. But it's the energy itself which produces the learning. In some of the more recent classes I've been trying to work on making a model of how to plan the transfer of educational objectives from the teacher and the teaching environment to the student. You really have student power when they start thinking about what it is that happens when you learn something. We tried this rather explicitly the last couple of times around and I think we did pretty good. In a sense it meant that the music theory was kind of a cover; what was really being taught in class was learning to learn. How to become conscious of yourself, aware of how you are now, and how to store that awareness so that you can compare it to where you are later on. The act of comparison is normally called evaluation. It's all split up into little boxes; in the individual student it isn't split up into little boxes, though, it's a continuous energetic process. And all growth processes have the same shape. So in trying to work on this learning theory, I am interested in the effect that a learning theory can have if it is made explicit to students and they are allowed to participate in its imput so that they can develop their own ideas of what they do when they become different.

A certain confidence must be built up, though, confidence enough to brave the confusion of "not knowing."

There are basically two ways to reduce uncertainty in a world of uncertainty. The first one is to use an oracle; the second one is to play a game. In order to use an oracle you have to believe in the oracle, otherwise you'll be just as confused as before. So in consulting an oracle like the I Ching, the prime requisite is that you ask the right question so that you'll be able to understand the answer.

A game situation, which approximates most of our normal level of learning, reduces uncertainty by limiting meaning from all possible meanings that an activity could have. You play by rules which are arbitrary. Now there are three postures that you can take with respect to a game that is going on. You can play according to the rules everyone has agreed upon; you can refuse to play completely, in which case you will be rejected; or you can make up your own rules, and then have two sub-choices. You can make them look superficially like the game moves everyone else is making and people will think you are playing their game when in fact you are playing a different one, or you can make up your own game and people will think you are not playing the game at all. Music is a subject which is kind of off in the corner where people don't notice it too much if you start making up your own rules and living by them. I've approached it this way, hoping to establish models by which other subjects can be approached—things like mathmatics, spelling, and social studies.

How do you specifically apply this to your own game of music theory, the Bead Game?

It's hard to describe the Bead Game verbally, but it's a circular abacus. It shortcuts the need for verbal tools by being a graphic display. It's limited to a system of twelve tones, the chromatic scale that we have here in the West. I believe though that without too much trouble it could be extended to include systems of indefinite pitches. There are certain fixed properties of vibrating objects that are independent of culture operating wherever you are. If you listen to Tibetan monks singing, they still sing perfect pitch even though their music doesn't have twelve discrete tones in it. Even music of radically different cultures that don't have music theory as we understand it, is still subject to the laws of vibrating objects like your vocal cords and your hearing apparatus. Anything that vibrates regularly follows these laws. That property of vibrating objects is constant and can be used as the basis of a music theory which is universal.

Within any system, the properties of that system can be predicted by the interaction of the properties of vibrating objects and concepts such as symmetry. In the twelve tone system you get twelve equally distributed tones that can be written around a circle like a clock face. Twelve is a kind of magic number, it has a lot of factors, things can be divided into it equally. And it works out as a useful organizer for musical sounds because there are many patterns of symmetry that make learning how to manipulate such a system very easy. And the general principles, the patterns, the rules for making up rules for dealing with such a system can be given easily in a few minutes. It might take as long as a couple of days to prove rigorously the fundamental theorems and postulates of the system I'm working on now.

In working with the Bead Game, do you actually break down your thinking and really begin to think in a different way?

INTRODUCTION TO THE BEAD GAME

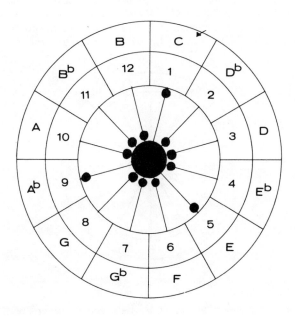

MAKE YOUR OWN BEAD GAME –

Materials:

12 straight pins

12 glass beads

1 piece of cork

1 piece of heavy cardboard

Directions:

Copy or cut-up the diagram. The two scales can be mounted on the cardboard.

Cut to the same size. Make each scale separately, so they can revolve around each other. Place the 12 pins in the cork, at the bottom, with the beads.

Then, attach the inside of the number scale to the heads of the pins with paste.

Place the game on the table so the letter scale may revolve around freely.

THE BEAD GAME

The BEAD GAME is a device which represents relationships in a system of twelve tones. The device consists of a circular number scale with the numbers one through twelve arranged at equal intervals around the circle, just like a clock face. In line with each number is a "spoke", or rod, on which a movable bead has been placed. Figure 1 shows the BEAD GAME in "rest" position.

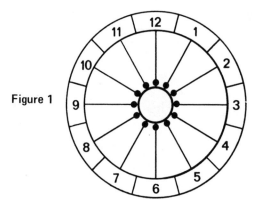

Figure 1

When a number (a note) is to be played, the bead which is in line with that number is moved so that it lies next to the rim of the wheel, nearest to the number scale. Figure 2 shows the numbers 1 and 9 in "play" position.

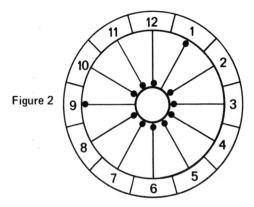

Figure 2

The number scale is divided into twelve degrees. One degree is the distance between two numbers which are next to each other. The relationship between any two numbers (and the tones they represent is expressed in terms of the number of degrees contained in the interval between them. Degrees may be counted in two directions: clockwise and counterclockwise. The letter 'D' signifies the number of degrees in the interval between any two numbers. In figure 3 the interval between one and two is D1, the interval between one and four is D3.

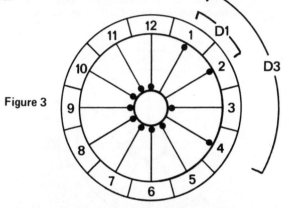

Figure 3

Since there are two ways to count the number of degrees in an interval, there are two possibilities for the size of the interval. If one possibility is <u>D</u>, the other possibility would be twelve minus D. Since either possibility describes the interval between numbers, D and 12—D are equivalent. Figure 4, the interval between one and eight may be described as either D5 or D7 with equal accuracy.

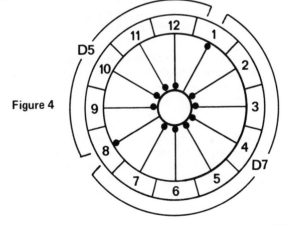

Figure 4

If one wished to relate the number system to the traditional letter names of the twelve notes, a sliding scale is added to the number scale. This chromatic sliding scale is added to the number scale. This chromatic sliding scale contains the twelve traditional letter names (C, C sharp, D, D sharp, E, F, F sharp, G, G sharp, A, A sharp, B) also arranged at equal intervals so that when the number "1" is in line with a letter, the assignment of the other eleven letter-number combinations is made as well. Figure 5 shows the chromatic sliding scale added to the Bead Game, with the letter "C" in line with the number "1". The chord 1-5-9 is seen to represent the augmented triad C—E—G sharp.

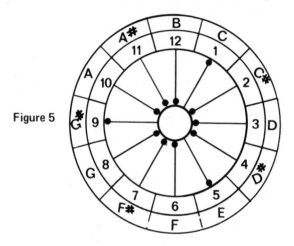

Figure 5

The symmetry of the chords, which is not very clear in standard notation becomes readily apparent using the Bead Game due to the circular arrangement of the twelve tones where any chord in which all intervals are equal will exhibit radial symmetry.

A chord is symmetrical when the numbers of which it is made up fall at equal intervals around the circle. Chords of two tones have two intervals; chords of three tones have three intervals.

SYMMETRICAL DIADS

The word 'Diad' means a 'group of two, a pair'. A symmetrical Diad (Abbrev. SD) divides the circle into two equal intervals of six degrees. D6 is the 'characteristic interval' of the symmetrical diad. The two Tones in an SD are diametrically opposite one another. Figure 1 shows the six different symmetrical diads. Any given number is a member of one and only one SD. This property does not hold true for any diad except the symmetrical diad.

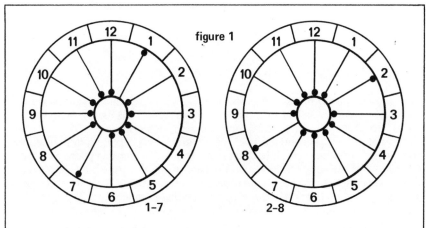

figure 1

1-7   2-8

RESOLUTION OF SYMMETRICAL DIADS

The movement of two tones one degree each +1, −1 is called 'resolution', and the first chord is said to <u>resolve</u> into the second.

The simplest case of resolution occurs when the chord is a symmetrical diad.

A symmetrical diad resolves when both of its tones move one degree in opposite directions. If one number moves up while the other moves down, the resultant diad will be a D4 (D8) diad. Any given SD may therefore resolve into two different new D4 diads. Starting with the SD 6–12, we may obtain the two D4 diads, 5–1 and 7–11. See figure 2.

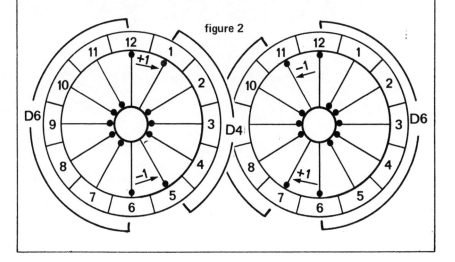

figure 2

CONNECTING D4 DIADS BY MEANS OF A 'COMMON TONE'

The second type of functional connection we will use is called connection by common tone. We will use this type of connection for D4 diads which result when an SD is resolved. D4 diads connect with each other and with D6 diads by common tone. A common tone is a number which is present in two success-ive chords. It is common to both chords. Any of the tones of chord may be chosen to be the common tone. On the bead game, this tone is left in the play position while the other tones are moved to rest position. The next succeeding chord will therefore contain this tone. A D4 diad (2-6 in figure 3) may con-nect by common tone with two new D4 diads (2-10, 6-10) and with two new D6 diads (2-8, 6-12).

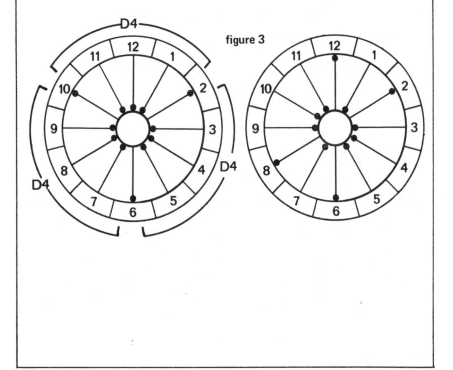

figure 3

CHORD PROGRESSIONS USING D6 AND D4 DIADS

We have now described two chord types and two types of connection. D6 diads resolve D4 diads; D4 diads connect by common tone with D4 and D6 diads.

Using these two chord types and these two functional relationships we can construct chord progressions of any desired length. Dashers are used in the progression in figure 4 to show common tone connections and the letter 'R' is used to show resolution.

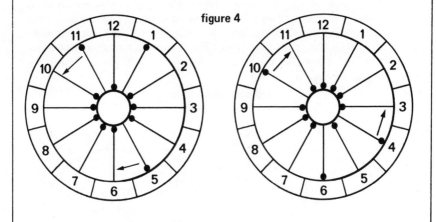

figure 4

THE PATTERN OF FUNCTIONAL RELATIONSHIPS

A Chord is a set of numbers arranged in a particular vertical order, i.e., a chord structure is a list consisting of numbers. A functional relationship is a rule which specifies that to each number in the chord structure (let us call it S_1) of the first chord, some number shall be added or subtracted to produce the next chord, S_2. In algebraic shorthand:

$$S_1 + F = S_2, \text{ where S and F are lists of numbers}$$

The function (F) can be as complex or as simple as desired. F may be only a "partial" rule, in that the treatment of some of the numbers in S_1 is not specified, but is optional. Two partial F's may be used at the same time. Here are the five rules, some of which are explained in the Diad Game, but here are seen at once as patterns of functional relationships.

COMMON TONE CONNECTION

F_1: Common Tone Connection means "Add <u>zero</u> to at least one of the numbers in S_1."

A common tone is a number which is present in two successive chords. It is 'common' to both chords. Any of the tones of a chord may be chosen to be the common tone. On the Bead Game, this tone is left in play position while the other tones are moved to rest position. The next succeeding chord will therefore contain this tone. Any of the other eleven tones may be added to this one to form a new chord.

For example: 10   9
                6 – 6   (6 is the common tone)
                2   1

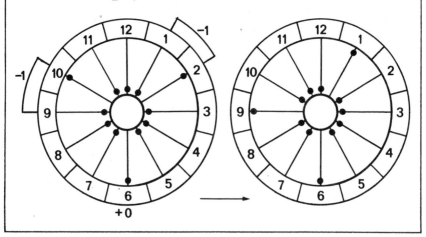

RESOLUTION

F_2: Resolution means "Add or subtract <u>one</u> from any two of the numbers in S_1."

Resolution is the movement of two tones of a chord, one clockwise and the other counterclockwise, a distance of one degree. Resolution is a procedure which applies to two tones of a chord, or in other words, to a <u>diad component</u> of a chord. There are six different sizes of diads, considering that (12 − D) is equivalent to D. When one number moves up and the other number moves down, the interval is increased or decreased by two degrees.

When a Symmetrical diad (D6 interval) is resolved in opposite directions, the two products are identical in structure: both are D4 diads. This property of symmetrical resolution sets the D6 diad apart from other diads. Since the two products are identical, resolution may be made to either D4 diad with identical effect.

The flexibility of the D6 diad in resolving to two possible D4 diads is preserved when the D6 is a component of a chord of more than two tones. The presence of the SD component is usually easily perceived by the listener, and chords with a D6 are readily distinguishable from chords without a D6 component.

ROTATION

F_3: Rotation means "Add or subtract <u>the same amount</u> from all of the numbers in S_1."

Rotation of a chord is achieved by adding or subtracting the same amount from all the tones of a chord. The new chord will be identical in structure to the original. Here are some examples of rotation, starting with the STD 1-5-8.

$$
\begin{array}{lll} \qquad & \begin{array}{ll} 8 + 2 & 10 \\ 5 + 2 = & 7 \\ 1 + 2 & 3 \end{array} & \qquad\qquad \begin{array}{ll} 8 - 1 & 7 \\ 1 - 1 = & 12 \\ 5 - 1 & 4 \end{array} \end{array}
$$

The descriptiveness of the term "rotation" may be easily visualized by performing this operation on the Bead Game.

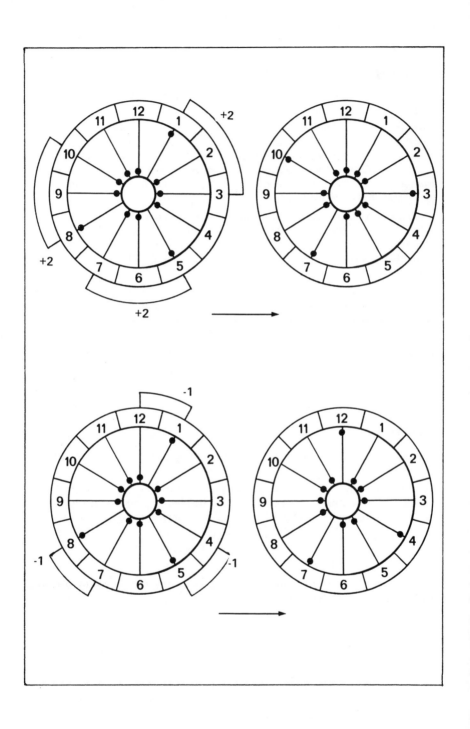

LEADING TONE

F_4: Leading Tone means "Add or subtract <u>one</u> from any one of the numbers in S_1. The new number thus obtained must be the root of S_2."

A chord has a root when two of its tones form a D5 interval. When the chord is set up on the H-Scale, the two tones forming the root are adjacent, and the tone on the counterclockwise side is conveniently called the root.

A <u>Leading Tone</u> is a tone which is D1 away from the root; that is, the leading tone is a tone of a chord which moves D1 in progressing to the next chord, and the tone to which it moves is the root of the next chord. Any one of the tones of a chord may be treated as a leading tone, but the analysis of a leading tone requires that both chords be examined.

A leading tone may move upward or downward in moving to a chord root.

UPSIDE DOWN AND BACKWARD

We have used four types of functional connection. They are: Resolution: two tones of a chord move one degree each; Common Tone: a selected tone is made a member of two or more successive chords; Rotation: all the tones of a chord move the same number of degrees in the same direction; Leading Tone.

It may be seen that the first three functions are reversible; that is, they work equally well forwards or backwards, therefore any progression which uses only these types of connection will be equally "logical" when it is played backwards the chords appearing in reverse order.

Moreover the notation we are using is symmetrical. [*Ed. note: The Bead Game Notation system, based on a six line staff is not explained here. This section is included to illustrate the total integrative structure that encompasses this system.*] When the staff is turned upside down, the numbers 1 and 7 do not change position. The other numbers change, in the following way: 2 becomes 12; 3 becomes 11; 4 becomes 10; 5 becomes 9; 6 becomes 8, and vice versa in each case. The distance from one and seven is preserved. This means that turning a chord upside down changes the numbers (other than 1 or 7), but the structure of the chord is not changed. All the symmetrical chords do not change at all; derivations and hybrids change tones but remain derivatives and hybrids.

The significance of all this is that any progression you write, using the suggested structures, functions and notation, will be a progression when played backwards upside down, or upside down and backwards.

Well, just the idea that you're free to make up your own rules about something is usually completely new to someone who's used to memorizing conventions that have been given. A convention is a rule, a rule which limits meaning. For example, the idea that you can only go clockwise in a monopoly game is a convention, it's printed on the sheet. You accept it, but you can imagine a monopoly game, and there are probably people who have thought of it, in which given a throw you have a choice of going forwards or backwards. It's an option that isn't in the rule book. It's a rule that you can make up if you want to. The fact that it isn't in the rule book isn't important.

You mean . . . there are no rules in music.

There are no given rules. The only restrictions are those which are given by the natural properties of vibrating objects. That is to say that some intervals will be perceived by the listener as more important than other ones; that's the only real limitation. I mean it's not really a limitation, it's a property of the system. Beyond that you are literally free to do anything that you want. What the Bead Game system does though, is give you a model of how to predict from deductive principles. So you're free to do anything you want, but it's better if you know what it's going to sound like before you actually play it. The idea of teaching music theory is to enable somebody to compose something.

At the risk of blowing your cover, I think there is even something more at stake. Music is traditionally considered by a lot of thinkers as the calculus of some higher harmony or universality.

No, I'm not afraid of blowing my cover. I think that the implications, as you say, grab the trunk. We're at the trunk; now, what is the actual system I am working with? It has to do with patterns which are generated by the interaction of the natural properties of vibrating objects which turn out to be extraordinarily simple, and symmetry which also turns out to be simple to grasp. The interaction is likewise very simple to use in understanding, prediction and control. But from the trunk the tree goes two ways. We can now go upward into the branches. I have received some material from a guy at SRI, who has been applying some of the principles of astrology and I Ching to theoretical systems analysis and computer programming. Pretty high powered I thought; it was very interesting. But I thought there was a level of symbol manipulation higher than that which needed to be explored and detailed. So I sat down and began to write out what I considered the rules for manipulating symbols in the abstract.

The first rule that I came up with was a definition of symmetry. That is the first thing that's really important in a system, because it really isn't systematic unless there is some symmetry in the system. That is, it can't be just linear and go on forever without ever repeating anything. The first rule for making up rules is that symmetry is invariant under conditions of transformation. I wrote a letter off to Fritz Kunz and The Center for Integrative Education, but didn't mention that at all, and the letter I got back from him said, "Symmetry is very important as it is invariant under conditions of transformation," almost the very words I had used. I said, this is a man who is on a very similar track. Can it be that this is not a coincidence? I feel that a lot of concepts—we're not even talking about concepts anymore; concepts are human constructs; perhaps principles or patterns is a better word—such as the interaction of symmetry with asymmetry have cosmic significance. And in discovering how to work with those patterns on this plane, you are in a sense plugging into the possibility of understanding things on a higher plane. And it's with that goal that Plato identified the three domains that we have now. Plato's division of man into three parts has been preserved, almost without change, in modern educational theory. But the last domain that he postulated has never been picked up, except by a few who are outside and who by and large reject the other domains. Very odd split.

The relation of harmonics to present-day science may be summed up in the simple proposition: not measure and number but measure and value. It is this which today's civilization must come to recognize if it is ever again to become a culture. And we do not mean measure here (science) and value there (religion, philosophy, art, etc.), but a regeneration of the scientific way of thinking from both Pythagorean approaches, hence a re-introduction of spiritual principles and laws (tone!) in to the heretofore purely haptical way of thinking (number). In this manner scientific thinking not only will acquire human warmth and human responsibility once more, but the realms outside this kind of thinking, such as religion and the arts, will again be joined with scientific thought through the symbols of the harmonical value-forms, and be lifted out of the regal isolation which made them matters for holidays and "leisure hours" only. The possibility of this regeneration is given in the primary phenomenon of the tone-number and the laws and principles flowing from it, and harmonics is the method by which this possibility may be transformed into reality.

—Hans Kayser, *from* Akroasis

Lose to Your Muse

Ed McClanahan and
Gurney Norman

Ed McClanahan and Gurney Norman are writers quite capable of teaching students how to write, but more important to this book, to the people they know, and to the world, they are each a rare sort of educator. If your writing is bad, they will support your ideas; if your ideas are bad, they will support your energy; and if your energy is bad, they will support whatever is left. A friend once said of Ed and Gurney, "They taught me to be an enthusiast rather than an analyzer." As such, they may be the best teachers around.

Well, how should we start this out?

Gurney: Ask us some of those questions.

They aren't really questions, they're topics. For one, I thought we could talk about personal journalism.

Ed: That suits *me*, but it might not suit Gurn.

Gurney: Well, I'll change it if it don't suit me. First thing I thought of when you were talking a minute ago, about writing and its connection to education, what came to my mind was what a terrible

time I've had trying to learn how to write, and what a terrible
time I've had tryin' to get some education . . .

Ed: To say nothin' of the terrible time I've had teaching him . . .
(Laughter)

Gurney: Yeah, Ed, we both suffered . . . but the fruit of our labors
is here, see, people comin' to interview us.

I always start thinking about how difficult it is to acquire a
voice: that's been the thing I've had an awful hard time doing.
I think that's probably a theme, the idea of coming to voice. It
depends upon growth, and if growth's education . . . they're probably the same thing . . . and it has a lot to do with identity.
I just turned thirty-four three or four days ago, and I remember
when I was *twenty*-four—by the time I was twenty-four, I had
a degree in journalism from the University of Kentucky and a com-
mission in the United States Army, and I'd spent a year in graduate
school at the University of Kentucky and a year as a writing fellow
in the Stegner program at Stanford, and had had teachers galore,
and I ended up twenty-four years old chronologically and about
twelve years old in all the important respects. It was about ten
years ago, when I was twenty-four, ostensibly a grown man, that
I began to get some real education. It's been a ten-year process
since then. I pretty much discount all the things that happened
before I came to California. I can't *really* discount them, but I
just don't remember. I just remember being a very ignorant, un-
confident person.

But I don't feel that way anymore; I feel like in the last ten
years something has changed, and that the source of that change
is education. Or identity. I'm beginning to have some sense of
who I am, and once you know that, you know who it is speaking,
so you can speak with some authority.

So voice to a writer is like identity to somebody else?

Gurney: Yeah, I think there's an equivalent to Voice in all the
arts . . . and fields. I think Willie Mays came to his voice, such
as it is—it's not the voice of language, but it's a mode of expression,

that thing that makes him good—, he came to his very early, twenty years ago, when he was a kid, a superstar. Some people arrive early, some late. In politics, you know, people arrive at their *stance*, their point of view. It has to do with coming to adulthood, and with the marshalling, the gathering of power.

Ed: You come to where you see yourself doing it, or, in the writer's case, you *hear* yourself doing it. I'm sure that when Willie Mays came into his "voice," into his maturity as an athlete, he came to a place where he was able to *see* himself doing what he was doing as he was doing it. I mean, it all happened at once, rather than in the retrospective way that bespeaks uncertainty and insecurity. Before that point, you have only perspective on your art, you aren't into it, identified by and in it. I'm sure, for instance, that Willie Mays never goes home and worries about the way he swung at the third pitch in the first inning that afternoon. It happens *then*, it happens on the spot.

How does this happen to a writer?

Ed: Well, I can tell you something about how it happened to *me*. There was a definite time in my life when I began to see that I was coming into my voice. I'd never had any sense of what a writer's voice was, in general, nor what my own particular voice was. I didn't understand what the word meant . . . until I was teaching freshman English up at Oregon State; I did that for four years, and the kind of teaching I was doing obliged me to learn grammar, which I hadn't really ever known anything about, though I had a Master's in English Literature. I hadn't studied grammar since eighth grade, and I didn't know shit from apple butter about grammar, so when I started out having to teach it, in this basic, stupid way, I simply had to go back to it, get into it and learn something about it myself. And at the same time that was happening, it just happened that I was working in the department up there with four remarkably good young poets, all four of whom were into lyricism in language in one way or another. And these guys were going around all the time talking about language in some cosmically different way that I'd ever *heard:* they talked about language the way a painter talks about paint . . . or a sculptor talks about stone. And I didn't quite understand what they meant, but . . . it was like, if you were a worker in a stone quarry, you got this new job in a stone quarry, and in all your off-hours you discover that you're hanging around a tavern where a bunch of sculptors are hanging around. That's what happened to me—I began to get a totally new concept growing in my head about what words were all about . . . what stone was all about. I'd tried to write a lot before, in college as an undergraduate, but it'd almost always been unsatisfying to me, finally, because the language was dead. I wasn't thinking then about language as I wrote, I was thinking about . . . oh, I don't know, *Story* or something. And when my writing first began to come alive, when I started doing it again after a year of being up in Oregon in that new situation, when my language began to take on a life, to be a thing that wasn't a *window* onto experience, but a living part of the experience itself . . . insofar as my writing's ever come alive, that's when it started to happen. That's where I began to get some sense of what the word "Voice" means.

Once you got that sense of language, how did that affect your education?

Ed: Well, I can tell you how it affected my *writing:* the immediate effect was that I got incredibly florid. The first quote successful unquote story that I ever did—a story that was published in *Contact* about ten years ago ["The Little-Known Bird of the Inner Eye"]—was a pretty good story, but the language is so exuberant from that discovery . . . I could never use one adjective where three would do. There's one sense in which the language in that story is rich, but it's also completely excessive. And some of that tendency is certainly still with me.

Gurney: The thing Ed's done in the last few years, when I've observed his writing, is to make use of what had amounted to a burden, a burdensome tendency to overwrite. He's been able to satirize himself, for one thing. And when you get so you can satirize yourself, it means . . . well, you know the phrase, "you get behind it," and that's a very useful . . . What do you call that?

Ed: Self-parody, I suppose, is what you mean.

Gurney: Well, there's *detachment*. That's a great moment in development, when detachment comes. Detachment and clarity come close to being synonyms, as I see it. Learning detachment is learning to see clearly, instead of seeing through various colored membranes.

Ed: Yeah, there are really three dimensions to this kind of growth: The writing I was doing as an undergraduate was one-dimensional, flat, and without self-awareness; and then when I learned about language, I acquired a second dimension, expressed in florid, over-ripe prose; and now there is a third dimension, which is me standing back looking at both of those two.

Gurney: The central theme running through Ed's essays in personal journalism the last few years is a sense of himself as a character. Getting on top of your work, you get on top of yourself too. When you see yourself being absurd, doesn't mean you have to go out and commit suicide; just because you see yourself being wise, you don't have to go and give yourself too many laurels on account of that. You don't have to take everything you see so seriously. Great humor has come into Ed's writing. Judy Rascoe used a great term for that, she talked about it as exuberance, a natural exuberance in Ed's writing. Ed's learned how to take great delight in himself, as just a complex guy.

Well, tempus did (as tempus will) fugit, and I survived my year at W & L and three more at Miami and (by the teensiest fraction of a shorthair) even a couple of quarters in grad school at Stanford. In 1956, thoroughly chastened by the hard use I'd suffered at the hands of Stanford's pernicious pedagogues (I did achieve a certain local notoriety in the English department for referring in a paper to John Donne's 'poetic suavity'; but that low order of fame is fleeting at best), I slunk back to Kentucky and enrolled at the University at Lexington, hoping somehow to escape the thorny groves of academe with something approximating a whole coat. And after a couple of years of posturing as a California beatnik-

cum-*intellectual* (*an act which constituted the only accomplishment I had to thank Stanford for*) *come to grace the hinterlands with his enlightened presence, I made it, I mean they actually awarded me a Master of Arts degree in English literature—though not before I'd gone down in the annals of the UK English department as the Only Grad Student Ever to Flunk the Mere Formality of the Master's Oral Exam. . .*

—Ed McClanahan, "Famous People I Have Known"

Gurney: I'm not sure what we're talking about right now. The thing I felt like saying a while ago, going into what Ed was saying, was about education—or my *experience* of the last ten years, which I think of as education. My post-college years have fallen very neatly into five two-year blocks, and each one of them has been a kind of graduate school. After I got a Bachelor's Degree, I hung around on college campuses two more years. I didn't get any advanced degrees, but I had the experience of being a graduate student; and then I went in the Army for two years and had a military experience, which was in some other direction than my studies in literature had taken me. When I left the Army, I went back to my home town in Hazard, Kentucky, and was editor of a weekly newspaper for two years, and got deeply involved in local social issues, political issues. And all the time I was going along trying to write these personal little short stories, and not finishing very many of them. Finishing a few. And finally what all this experience didn't have anything, overtly, to do with, was *me:* all the talk in the army was about the batallion and the company and the ongoing training; and all the talk in graduate studies was about Cree-ay-tive Writing, you know, and literary criticism and other writers. I couldn't find anybody to tell me anything about myself; and I didn't know enough to ask the question, I didn't know that I didn't know anything about myself. I wound up fleeing my newspaper job because it was too impersonal. I just roamed around for a couple years, living with friends, and at that point I began to run into people who would look at me, alone, and talk to me—very sophisticated people. And during those two years I had a summer job: for two consecutive summers I was a lookout in Oregon. I lived alone for fourteen weeks at a stretch in this lookout tower on a mountain peak, and all I did was just sit there, and in the process of watching out for forest fires, I just meditated. It was a moment of pure stillness, everything stopped. It was down in that time that all my busy-ness—whether an army officer, or an editor, or a student, all very, very *busy*—, for the first time in my adult life, I wasn't busy, I was just sitting there. In that time of stillness, a whole other direction in my education, in my growth began and I was into stuff no one could train me for. You know, you're *trained* to be a scholar, you're *trained* to be an army officer, you're *trained* to be a newspaperman . . . and none of that is education. So my experience got personal, I began to pay attention to my own insides, and it was at that point that I felt as if a true education was beginning for me; and the last four years have continued in that way . . . but anyhow, that's a radical education I've just described, I think, it's not an institutionalized one.

The little clean man on the end of the park bench is my grandfather, about twenty-five years ago.

The drifter on the other end is my father, who died in the Veterans Hospital in St. Louis, Missouri in 1962.

That's me between them, looking pensive, undecided, trying to figure out which way to go.

My father never did get straight which way he should go, but my grandfather never had the slightest doubt.

That's why he was such a clean little man, and my father not so clean.

My grandfather was an American, you see. And when you're an American, and you know that you are, know it for sure, and can trust absolutely the things you know, there's never any doubt which way you must go.

You go west.

Americans know that about themselves with such assurance they get a marvelous clean feeling up and down their spines every time the sun goes down.

—Gurney Norman, "On a Park Bench with Two Ghosts,
One Cleaner Than the Other"

In this personal writing, you must get a sense of the non-personal, universal aspect of things, from the language. I'm really interested—of course anybody is if he wants to apply those universal aspects to his life—in how those can fit into the writing.

Gurney: There are a lot of Zen aspects in the thing we're talking about. You know that Chinese poet Han Chan, the ole mystic who lived on the mountain, and all he did was run around and act foolish, and just snicker and laugh at practically everything, including himself. Everything was funny, y'know, everbody's airs, everbody's pretensions, were all absurd to him, including his own.

There's a section in my own book where this character, this young man named Divine Right, is having a kind of nervous breakdown. The action of the story takes him underground, and the passage is a metaphor for a kind of psychic death. The theme of a descent into the underworld, into the subterranean, and then a subsequent re-emergence into the world again, is a theme all cultures have produced in legends and mythologies.

I don't think that professional educators would agree that spiritual enlightenment is the ultimate goal of education, but that's because most professional educators are interested in training, not education. I can't separate the artistic impulse from the religious impulse. I guess that's why I wound up becoming no more radical, politically, than I did. Seems to me that if you're an artist, you inevitably become concerned, at some point, with ideas of infinity, and you wind up talking about God. It's not a question that most of the Hot Contemporary American writers seem interested in.

Admitting then that Zen and poetry overlap to some extent, let us ask the question, is there anything which is poetical but has no Zen in it? Are there some non-poetical elements in Zen? . . . The enemies of poetry,—vulgarity, sentimentality, romance, indifference, lack of humour—, these are the enemies of Zen. Yet Zen, like poetry, like humour, turns our stupidity into interest, our falsity into a revelation of truth, our motiveless malignity into meaningful 'love,' our defeat into victory, Thus are confirmed the paradoxical words of Socrates, 'Think this certain, that to a good man no evil can happen, either in life or in death.' This 'good man' is the man of Zen, the man of Poetry.

—*R.H. Blyth, "Zen and Poetry I" from* Zen and
Zen Classics, Vol. 5

Ed: Anybody's natural voice is beautiful, y'know, that's the point of that Found Poetry essay. All language really *is* poetry just because all poetry is, is language. I mean, where language is less than beautiful is where it's falsified somehow, where people are trying to do something that's not theirs, that doesn't come straight out of them . . . You find out what's you, and then you write *that*. I don't think you do it by *writing after* what's yours; you do it by *considering* what's yours.

And then once you do that, how do you change because of that?

Ed: You begin to discover what your own dimensions are. You do that by understanding your own voice.

The danger though, I think, is of getting lost, and of not recognizing the truth or falsity of what you're saying. I was going to ask—every writer must have a self-checking device, a quality-control device . . .?

Ed: *Everything* is true, is the thing. Finally, you just can't make judgments like that.

I didn't mean it in a judgment sense.

Ed: Well, you're talking about the risk you take when you give yourself over to this *intuitive* process where, as Gurney says, you Lose to Your Muse. So you get . . . you just can't make that kind of consideration.

Yeah, but some things that come out from the inside just wouldn't be worth writing about, because they're not the real stuff.

Gurney: I'm not sure I know the answer to that. Sure there's a certain amount of arrogance involved anytime someone goes off and does something arty and then takes up somebody else's time with it. I don't think there's any pat thing to say about that.

Ed: No, there ain't.

Gurney: Well, now, there's arrogance in it; and there's talented arrogant people and untalented arrogant people.

Ed: (laughing) We happen to be among the former. Here. Those of us here together. Today.

Gurney: I believe in rules. I think they're important—rules of grammar, rules of life, rules of law.

Ed: Narrative structure.

Gurney: Everything. I think it's unfortunate that this kind of rap usually leads into some kind of terribly polarized thing.

Ed: The thing about rules are . . . (pause; laughter) . . . *is*—

Gurney:"The thing about grammatical rules are . . ."

Ed: The thing about grammatical rules *ain't* . . . no, I think you have to understand that what rules mean is that there's *order* in language. They're not meant to be a set of restrictions at all, no more than molecular physics are a restriction on the way one's body moves. You don't study physics in order to learn your limits; you study physics in order to understand the dynamics of the system. That's what grammar is, the physics, or the mathematics of language. And knowing math doesn't mean that you have to *count* everything.

   . . . He felt his life go out, and turn into a fish with gills and scales and fins and tail, tempted by a powerful light that dangled from his brain. The light scared him, but he nosed around it, lured and terrified. Against his will he nibbled at its edges. As soon as his lips touched the light, a three-pronged hook snagged his throat and yanked him up. Blood filled his throat and ran out of his gills and eyes and asshole and spilled upon the sand. He struggled to ease the pressure of the hook against his flesh, but the fisherman only laughed and dangled him up and down. At last when he could stand no more the fisherman gave the

line a jerk and ripped D.R.'s tongue out by the roots and dropped him
to the sand. Words rose up in him to protest but they could get no farther
than his throat. Words that started deep inside him lifted through his
system to collide and fall part in heaps of jumbled abc's. Words he'd
said in childhood came charging into words he'd heard old preachers say
in sermons long ago, words of preachers, words of teachers, words mysterious
kinfolk uttered over Sunday chicken dinners into words he'd muttered to
himself in saying who he was and might become all crashed against the
roadblock and piled up in a grave of words as dry and hard as bones.
D.R. picked up a bone shaped like the letter W. He smelled it, licked
his tongue across it, held it to his ear. He tried an O, and R, and
a broken D, but they were all the same. Dead. Dead. All the words
were dead, not one had lived to tell what happened, none survived that
knew the tale. Tell it! said the fisherman, but all he could do was cry.
Tell it! said the fisherman, but all he could do was cry. The fisherman
cursed and roughly kicked D.R. back into the river. The water scalded
his wound as it mixed with blood and made a soup for bones of broken
letters D.R. clutched at for support to keep from drowning.
                                   —*Gurney Norman. from* Divine Right's Trip

Non-writers also get some sense of a muse in their lives, which
can be applied by expressing it somehow. How does inspiration
relate to your writing?

Ed: If I ever saw anyone genuinely inspired, it was Gurney doing
that book [*Divine Right's Trip*], especially at the end of it. That
was a wild process to observe.

Let me tell you one story. I have a friend who's a writer,
Haven O'More. I was asking him what it felt like for him
to write, but then somehow we drifted away and I told him
about this time I was in Big Sur, climbing up a big rock
in the surf. I was climbing up one side, the shore side, and
as I reached my head over this one ridge—it was really lucky
I was holding on—this gigantic wave, I mean just GIGANTIC,
completely engulfed me. I was about thirty feet high; it would
have been just about all over for me but I held on and kept
going, over the other side, and found out that it was about

the worst ascent I could have chosen. The rest was straight
up. I was scared out of my mind, but I just kept going straight
up like a mountain goat until I got to the top. When I got
to the top, I was tingling all over—just up and down my
hands, all through my whole body this incredible tingle, after
going through that . . . and Haven stopped me right there
and said, "That's what it's like when I write!"

Gurney: Well, I couldn't say that that's what it's like when I write
every word, but I'm ready to say that I have some idea what inspired
writing is. And I think what it is, it's when you aren't censoring
it as it happens, you aren't playing that . . .

Ed: "What's the *New York Times* Book Critic going to say about
this sentence?"

Gurney: No, not even that. You're beyond saying, "I'm not capable
of doing this." Like there are stories of ninety-pound women who
lift up the tail end of a Ford off their children who're being crushed.
She didn't pause to say, "This can't be done." So it's in that category,
and it's beyond self, y'know, it's beyond who you are, it's beyond
the part of you that has a name. That wasn't Sam Yanes scrambling
up that rock, that was a human mortal operating out of survival
instincts. The part of me that bears my name is maybe ten percent
of who I really am.

Ten per cent? (Laughter)

Gurney: This body of mine is a life-support system for my consciousness, and when you get direct access to your subconscious,
there's the writing. I call that "writing from the demon"; *that's*
the thing you're operating right out of. And that ten-per-cent person,
who bears the name, the history, and the experience of Gurney,
is off somewhere suspended for the moment. This is connected
to what I said about identity, about coming to identity; what I
just *now* said is about abandoning identity. I cain't help it if it
sounds like a contradiction.

Yeah, I see that. It's not a contradiction.

What in fact are you, essentially and not accidentally; that is to say, 'in yourself', and not as butcher, baker, or candlestick maker? You cannot profitably try to be yourself unless you are sure that you can answer that question.

—*Lord Northbourne, "With God all things are possible"*
from Looking Back on Progress

Gurney: I think it has to do with heroic behavior, of all kinds. What you said, Ed, about Willie Mays a while ago—well, Willie's not *worrying* about it, you know? Willie's *arms* and *shoulders* and *legs* and *torso* hit that home run; if an athelete's out there still arguin' about it in his mind, he's not going to be very good. Guy here lately jumped seven feet six. He couldn't believe it. What *was* it that jumped seven feet six? Like, heroes are mortal people, everyday guys who get into extraordinary circumstances which summon them to extraordinary behavior. You wouldn't ever *volunteer* for the circumstances you get put in, but you get into a situation that means, you just got to shit or get off the pot, one or th'other; and the hero goes ahead and comes through with whatever it is.

That getting into a real circumstance that *insists* that you act, why that's a real-life thing. And you perform heroically: you go ahead on and deliver the baby, because there's just no way to *not* deliver it. If this all has anything to do with formal education, it's this: most classroom circumstances are *un*real circumstances, they're vacuums. There's no *occasion*, no opportunity in there to be heroic.

. . . Zen means doing anything perfectly, making mistakes perfectly, being defeated perfectly, hesitating perfectly, having stomach-ache perfectly, doing anything, perfectly or imperfectly, PERFECTLY. What is the meaning of the PERFECTLY? How does it differ from perfectly? PERFECTLY is in the will; perfectly is in the activity. Perfectly means that the activity is harmonious in all its parts, and fully achieves its proposed end. PERFECTLY means that at each moment of the activity there is no egoism in it, or rather, that our ego works together with the attraction and repulsion of the Egoism of the nature within and without us . . .

Our failure of misjudgment is that of nature, which never hopes or despairs, but keeps on trying to the end, like Bruce's spider, which failed to fall at last, or like Alfred's cakes, which succeeded in being burnt to a cinder.
—*R.H. Blyth, Preface to* Zen and Zen Classics, Vol. 5

Gurney: I guess finally you end up talking about what genius is, what talent is. I think it has something to do with how naturally a human being is tuned into large processes around him. There's a way in which an artist is a kind of funnel, that in *fact* he receives certain . . . he receives from somewhere else—it's probably from within himself somewhere—he receives a poem out of the sky, the Lord sends it to him. I love talk like that. It's like, you don't *make* it happen, you *let* it happen; at the same time, I know that there are times when you have to make it happen.

Ed: Right, it sure doesn't mean you don't have to work at it.

Gurney: Yeah, there are a lot of apparent contradictions. It's like . . . I been reading about Daniel Boone. The thing that's special about Boone, the reason he did what he did and his father didn't do it was because Daniel was prepared. He was prepared by his experience, by the lessons he learned from the time he was old enough to walk. His father was a farmer, had all the skills of a farmer, but it's not the farmers who become the Long Hunters—that is to say, who go into the unknown, into the wilderness, and scout it out, establish a clearing. Well, O.K., so there was no one in Boone's father's generation who was capable of doing what Daniel did as a young man. Daniel was in his thirties when he did his heroic deed, and his preparation had continued and his skills improved: he was good with an axe, he was strong, he had endurance, he could walk long distances, he was an expert marksman, he was an expert at identifying signs around him, he was courageous, he wasn't a brutal man . . . but, see, all these things were special skills, and he was placed in a unique circumstance: he lived on the edge of the frontier at a special moment. The opportunity was there, the *summons* was there: to *perform*, artistically. He did it because he was capable of it. I hope I'm setting this up clearly as a metaphor for an artist. You begin to think about all the things that a writer has to be. He has to be able to use language competently, have a good ear, he's got to have some philosophy—he's got to *understand* his material—he's got be seasoned, he's got to have experience with death, with tragedy. So there's a long period of learning that goes on. It's preparation, it's virtue, hell yes!—all cultivated things. Writers can have mentors for some of these things, but they also finally come up against that thing that makes them unique . . . Voice, which translates into style, that's uniquely one's own. I think an artist *is* a hero. A hero is someone who answers a summons from the gods. And I think that's the difference between being an artist and being simply a professional writer.

I'm sure that an artist's work is something like Daniel Boone stalking through the forest completely attuned to every sound; it's a precarious time, and a lot is at stake. A man's life. You hear a little twig break over there, a leaf rattle here, the wind blowing up there . . . you hear all that, and you can't stop and write an essay about why or why not you're going to respond to that particular twig. You just do or don't, because your whole process is alive to it and considering it, your total brain . . . you're making use of your whole process instead of just your logic, which is only one tool of your mind.

'When I talk about musicians, I'm talkin' about people who make music, *not just people who are technically perfect. 'Music' bein' That Thing Which Gets You Off, I mean that's just my definition of that word. And when you're playin' and Gettin' Off that way, it's like when you're drivin' down a road past an orchard, you know, and you look out and at first all you can see is just another woods, a bunch of trees all jumbled up together, like there's no* form *to it, it's chaos. But then you come to a certain point and suddenly—zing! zing! zing!—there it* is, *the* order, *the trees all lined up perfectly no matter which way you look, so you can see the real* shape *of the orchard! I mean you know what I mean? And as you move along it gets away from you, it turns into chaos again, but now it doesn't matter, because now you* understand, *I mean now you* know *the secret.'*

—*Jerry Garcia, as quoted in Ed McClanahan's*
"Grateful Dead I Have Known"

Ed: I get completely lost in the intricacies of making sentences when I'm writing. I love long, intricate sentences that have a kind of tension built into their structures. Whenever I write a subject and then intersperse a bunch of clauses and phrases between that and the verb, I do it with a complete awareness that when I suspend *that* verb *that* way, when I put it off, a certain tension builds up. Structural tension. It's just like when you're building something with an Erector set: you build a beam out and out and out, and you can feel just how many links you can add on to it before it gives, before it all collapses. And if you can create that kind of tension in the reader's mind, then you get internal energy, you know, kinetic potential in the words, . . . and it's really a trip to get involved in. I just get totally involved in the sheer mechanics, the *machinery* of a sentence. I get stoned on puns, on internal resonances, on the way words bang up against one another, both in terms of their sounds and their meanings. All the layers of their meanings. I like old words, and ornate words. I like the process that goes in the direction of involution, as opposed to the direction of outward, expansive kind of writing, which is probably more characteristic of Gurney than of me.

So there I am in September 1970, early morning, and I'm hurrying home to California to write about the Grateful Dead (I've been at this quite a while, you understand) after a three-week hiatus back east, barreling along in my big Dodge camper all alone through the everlasting vasty reaches of central Iowa, on a back road somewhere forty miles in some direction or other from Cedar Rapids, and it's raining like a cow pissing on a flat rock, a cold, driving rain that chills me even with the camper's heater ramming hot air up both pantlegs, and beside me on the hump of the engine's housing are spread my Official Accuracy Reporter's Notebooks filled with three-week-old runic scribblings . . . and several yellowing copies of Rolling Stone *featuring articles about the Dead, and my little portable stereo tape recorder, and five tape casettes of the Dead's albums, and—here comes the weird part—on my head I'm wearing, Buck Rogers-like, an enormous set of super-powerful stereo headphones plugged into the recorder, and the volume is turned up full blast and the Dead's 'Turn On Your Lovelight' is crashing against my eardrums, Pigpen snarling 'turn it on! turn it* on!' *into both ears at once, and I'm bouncing ecstatically in*

my seat and hammering the heels of my hands on the steering wheel to
Bill the Drummer's surging, nineteen-to-the-dozen rhythms while the guitars
scream as loud as locomotive whistles, you could knock my eyeballs off
my face with a broomstick, and now a new image swirls to mind and
shapes itself, the interior of my skull has somehow become the interior
of the Fillmore West, San Francisco's onetime Carousel Ballroom, this
cavernous old relic of a pleasure palace amidst whose tawdry elegance
our forebears forbore Guy Lombago and Shep Fields and His Rippling
Rhythm that we might live to dig the Dead, my throat and tongue the
Fillmore's threadbare maroon-carpeted lobbies and stairwells and my teeth
its curlicuing roccoco plaster balustrades and my brainpan the grand ballroom
itself, my medulla oblongata its vaulted ceiling festooned with heavily
sagging billows of silvery-gray asbestos damask, and there are three thousand
dope-crazed Dead fans crouched haunch-to-haunch in the darkness on the
immense dancefloor of my mind, while at the far end of the great chamber,
onstage, dwarfed beneath the high curved bleached-white bandshell that
is the inner surface of my forehead, the Grateful Dead are Getting It
On, a demon-driven suicide squad of assassins under the harsh command
of the arch-brigand Pigpen ('turn it on! jes a leetle bit hi-eee-yer!'),
a murderous little band of renegades, savages, Tartars in cowboy mufti,
Angels of Death armed not with three supercharged guitars and a set
of traps but with three choppers and a mortar, mercilessly laying waste
to the shrieking, writhing mass of defenseless supplicants spread beneath
them, and against the backs of my eyeballs the giant lightshow screen
behind the bandstand is ablaze like the night sky above a battlefield with
the garish lightning of their fusillade, it is more than just a massacre,
it is a by-god apocalypse hurtling along right here inside the fragile
eggshell of my skull at seventy miles an hour through the Iowa monsoon,
the incredible cacophony of it thrumming in my blood and beating wildly
against the backs of my eyes, mounting and mounting and mounting until
it peaks out at about eleven million megadecibels and Pig screams
'yeeeeeeeeee-o-o-o-o-o-o-o-owwwwwwwwwwwwwww!' and barks
'And leave it on!' and within the headphones there descends an abrupt
and wondrous stillness, a silence made infinitely deeper and more profound
by the absence not merely of the Dead's righteous racket but of all sound,
the headphones baffling out even the engine's roar along with the slap-
slap-slap of the wipers and the steady suck of tires on the flooded roadbed,
as if the whole wet world were inexplicably and without warning stricken

mute, and as the wipers streak the veil of water on the windshield, I
see, standing stalwart by the lonely Iowa roadside like Heaven's own herald,
an enormous billboard, sky-blue, with great thick square white letters
proclaiming, for no good reason at all,

TIME ENDS
ETERNITY WHERE

and even as the windblown water sheets the glass again, blurring, then
fracturing the image beyond all intelligence, I hear Jerry Garcia begin
the next song on the tape, his voice rising sweet and clear and plangent
into the silence,

You know Death don't
Have no mercy
In this land . . .

Ed McClanahan, from "Grateful Dead I Have Known"

Gurney: There's another factor which is relevant here, though I
don't know just yet how it's relevant. 'Minds me of the time last
summer when me and Wendell Berry and Wendell's son Den were
walking up Cane Run to look at a nest where some young buzzards
were. And Den, who's nine, got all sweaty and hot and impatient.
We just walked on up in this field, and Den was whining and
so forth to go home, and Wendell got mad after a while and said,
"Hush Den! If you'll be quiet, you'll know why we *came* here."
I guess I feel that way in starting to talk about folk stuff, about
what is a folk community? and what is folk art? and how it's
connected to what we're talking about. A folk skill or a folk craft
is by definition not refined. Some things get so goddamned refined
that they're pretty lifeless, pretty far removed from any kind of
ground. Ground is the source of stuff: folk communities live close
to the ground and folk craftsmen are uneducated folk, and yet
they're possessed of great skill and wisdom and artistic talent. Me
and Ed and Wendell know this chairmaker in Kentucky, who makes
beautiful chairs, and he works only with his hands, Wendell asked
him one time, "Chester, how did you learn to make these chairs?"
And Chester said, "It come to me from my ancestors." He doesn't
even much *remember* learning about it; oh, he did have an uncle,
who was the representative of his ancestors, who taught him specific

skills. But you know, Chester is the foremost chairmaker in the country as far as I know. Oh, I'll just ramble. You know another thing I thought of lately—you see, I'm claiming that *Divine Right's Trip* is a folk tale. I think of it as a folk tale and I got some very literary reasons for thinking that. But I mean I think of it as a home-made book; and I'm kind of anticipating reviewers, hostile reviewers talking about some of the roughness in the writing, which I know is there, and what I have already prepared to say is that I'd like to be able to not write the way Johnny Cash can't sing. Because the thing about Johnny Cash is he can't sing and the fact is, he's a fantastic singer. There's that *source* in him, that power, and I think it's a folk source. That's the direction I feel myself going in . . .

Ed: I, on the other hand, would rather be a singer who *can* sing. (Laughter)

Gurney: Well, Ed's an aristocrat, see, and I'm a peasant. (Laughter)

But I don't consider the concept of Folk to have anything to do with The Common People.

Ed: Yeah, that certainly is what *Divine Right's* all about.

Gurney: Right. The most viable folk thing happening in this country is happening with middle-class kids looking for a folk heritage, and, unable to find it, trying to create it. I think that's one of the best things about the freak community. Again I don't want to sound like what I'm looking for is illiteracy; my predecessors, I mean the people in the direction I want to go, are very literate people—Yeats, Frank O'Connor, James Joyce—, those writers got into Gaelic language and folk legends and so on. I'm interested in doing something like the same thing with the folk culture that I came from, the Appalachian hillbilly communities. But I'm not sure how this connects with education.

It connects directly with education.

Gurney: Connect it.

Because what it has to do with is transmission, and transmission is education.

Gurney: OK. I can dig that.

Well, for instance, if you look at sacred art—if you look at temples in India, or at mosques in Iran, or at Gothic cathedrals, they're all different, peculiar to a particular folk (not meaning people), but they're all . . . they can't be duplicated by any other folk. You can't build an Indian temple here, you just can't. And it's not because it's out of place, you just can't do it. And of course all these sacred architectures use the same principles. It's like asking Sufi writers now, "Why study the Red Indian?" Well, they do it anyway, because it broadens their knowledge of their own heritage; in any case, their own tradition. Learning has to come from transmission, from tradition, and that's why all the Sufi sects say that they come from direct transmission from Mohammed, and although they might not be literally related, they do, in fact, because of transmission, transmission's there, and it's there through something, call it folk, folk's a good word . . . "Sufi" means folk.

Gurney: Does it? That's fantastic. I think that what's gone wrong in the United States is the loss of that very orderly system of transmission. We tried to institutionalize that system, and it can't be institutionalized. The simplest way to say it is that we've tried to make schools take the place of parents. How many sons learn anything from their fathers any more? Hardly any. For two reasons, the main one being that their fathers don't *know* anything, because they've been very eager to cut loose, y'know, from the place that they come from, from the people that they come from. That's why most parents are pretty damn dull to their children. That nature of work has gotten so abstract and mysterious, and even apparently pointless, how could a son be interested in what his father does? I don't know how you reverse that destructive trend. I guess that's what education of the kind you're interested in is looking for.

Writing can be a transmission. Why write? If you're a good writer then first of all it's your God-given duty to be a folk writer, so to speak. It's your duty to transmit.

Gurney: I'm a native of Appalachia; I grew up in Perry County, Kentucky. My father was a coalminer, all my mother's people were coalminers. We've all got blown out of Kentucky, and all have become exiles. My family, and all the families I knew in the Fifties, were exiles to Ohio and Indiana and Illinois. Since World War II the culture we were born into there in the Kentucky mountains has been sundered. The thing I've been very slowly coming to over the years, and I had to leave Kentucky to come to it, is a sense of . . . well, first of all the slow discovery of the story, of the legend of the people, the legend that accounts for my family and my ancestors. I've been trying to resurrect that for years, been trying in every way I can to get the story in my mind. A lot of it's already in there; I have a very retentive memory and my mind is just loaded with a sense of life as it was in the late Thirties, for example, before every family had a car, and so forth, and I've learned a lot from my grandparents. I was raised by my grandparents pretty much, all four of my grandparents lived until I was 30 years old, and I talked to them much; so my sense of what *their* life was like in the late nineteenth century is very strong. As a writer I feel special as hell, because I know a story . . . that's not only about an individual, it's about a *tribe*. I feel like I'm the bearer of a legend. I've inherited some fantastic images and they're all in my head. What I want to do is transmit the contents of my head; I feel like my head is a seed loaded with pollen. The pollen is simply what I remember and what I know. It's a fantastic way for a writer to think of himself, because you feel part of a community, you see.

The thing that modern fiction's been about since the war has been despair and alienation and the idea of one poor individual feeling depressed because suddenly he realizes he's alone in the universe, that existential stuff and, you know, *fuck* it, I don't feel that way, I feel *surrounded* by clan, families, ancestry, and the thing that I *know* is what story I'm in. All the di-verse elements in the United States are trying to recover their *story*. What it blasts apart is the myth of the American melting pot; like America wants to melt everbody, turn everbody into a bland, Menlo Park, S.R.I. [Stanford Research Institute], twelve-thousand-dollar-a-year man with no *history*. Well, there's something very strong and powerful, some instinctive drive let loose in the country now which is an appetite for the *story*.

Of course you're talking about reclaiming birthright.

Gurney: Right! Exactly! It's got to be reclaimed in the mind before it can be reclaimed physically. Actually, I'm not sure it can be reclaimed physically any more, it'd probably be a psychological reclaiming of birthright. I'm really knocked out by how you connect that to education. You see education as transmission, the passing on of knowledge. That's far out.

Notes on Weave Material

New School News Blues
New Schools Exchange Newsletter, $10/year, 301 East Canon Perdido, Santa Barbara, California 93101.

Freely Naked At Pacific High
Domebook II, $4.00, Pacific Domes, Box 279, Bolinas, California 94924.

Rodent Cages, Trundle Wheels, and Other Basic Materials
Big Rock Candy Mountain, Education and Classroom Materials, $3.00, 540 Santa Cruz, Menlo Park, California 94025.

The Sense of Sharing
Sharing, $5.95, Freestone Publishing Company, 440 Bohemian Highway, Freestone (Sebastopol), California 95472.
Rasberry Exercises, Freestone Publishing Company.

Lose To Your Muse
Famous People I Have Known, Word-Wheel Books, 540 Santa Cruz, Menlo Park, California.
Big Rock Candy Mountain, Education and Consciousness.
Zen and Zen Classics, Vol. 5, R.H. Blyth, Japan Publications Trading Company, 1255 Howard Street, San Francisco, California 94103.
"Divine Right's Trip", *Last Whole Earth Catalog,* 558 Santa Cruz, Menlo Park, California 94025.

The Bead Game
The Bead Game, Portola Institute, 540 Santa Cruz, Menlo Park, California 94025
Akroasis, Hans Kayser, Plowshare Press, P.O. Box 2252, Boston, Massachusetts 02107.